# A Comprehensive Guide to Training Aggressive and Reactive Dogs
## Transforming Aggression

## Morgan Wells

Dream Publishing Pty Ltd

First edition 2024

# Disclaimer

The information provided in this book is intended for educational purposes only and is not a substitute for professional advice from a qualified dog trainer, behaviorist,or veterinarian.

Every dog is unique,and while the techniques discussed may help in managing aggression and improving behavior, they may not be suitable for all dogs.

If your dog displays severe or dangerous aggression, it is recommended that you seek the assistance of a certified professional behaviorist or trainer. The author and publisher are not responsible for any injuries or damages resulting from the application of the information in this book.

# Contents

# Chapter 1

# Introduction

D og aggression and reactivity cause many dog owners distress and confusion. A dog's aggressive behavior—barking, lunging at strangers, or biting—can be upsetting for the owner and others.

These behaviors might make it hard to take a dog out in public, entertain guests, or just enjoy a dog's company.

Although difficult, hostility and reactivity don't have to be lifetime issues. Even dogs with serious behavioral disorders can learn safe, controlled responses with proper training, patience, and dedication.

Dog aggression and reactivity are essential because they threaten safety. A vicious dog can hurt humans, animals, and itself.

Fearful and responsible owners of aggressive dogs wonder when their dog will attack. This makes the home tense, and the dog may be confused by its family members' reactions. In addition to safety problems, there are social implications. Bad preconceptions and anxieties about certain breeds of aggressive dogs can perpetuate cycles of cruelty and misunderstanding of dogs.

Dogs who are aggressive or reactive reduce the quality of life for both the dog and the owner. Simple things like walking, playing in the park, or hosting guests become stressful.

This stress makes the dog behave poorly and weakens the owner-dog link, causing irritation, loneliness, and even feelings of failure. Aggressive dog owners may feel judged by people who don't understand dog behavior.

This book helps owners and trainers understand that hostility and reactivity can be changed. A prevalent misperception regarding aggressive dogs is that their behavior is ingrained and unchangeable. Not true. Some dogs are genetically predisposed to violent behavior, but they can learn to act differently. Another myth is that aggressive dogs are "bad" dogs, but the truth is more complicated. Dog aggression has many causes, but training and behavior modification may fix most of them.

Well-meaning owners often utilize punishment-based tactics, which fail to address the fundamental causes of aggression and can worsen the situation. Punishment often teaches dogs to suppress their normal actions without correcting the problem, causing tension and frustration. This may lead to a more serious attack.

This book emphasizes positive reinforcement to manage and improve violent behavior in a compassionate manner.

Instead of punishing a dog, positive reinforcement rewards excellent behavior. It helps the dog associate calm and regulated behavior with favorable results. Besides positive reward, the book discusses behavior modification, which involves finding aggression triggers and desensitizing the dog to them. Safety will be a primary emphasis during training to protect the dog and others.

Understanding Aggression/Reactivity

Aggression and reactivity are commonly misconstrued, therefore it's crucial to understand the difference before learning how to train aggressive behavior. Behaviors designed to harm are aggression. This can include snarling, biting, snapping, or charging. Aggression frequently stems from fear, frustration, or the urge to defend oneself or a region.

Reactivity, however, is heightened emotional responses to certain stimuli. Reactive canines may bark, lunge, or become obviously distressed when faced with other dogs, loud noises, or unknown people. Reactivity is a dog's response to something overpowering or dangerous, unlike aggression. Aggression and reactivity may look similar, but their reasons are distinct, therefore the training strategy should too.

Aggression in dogs has many causes. Fear is a common reason. A scared or threatened dog may act violently to defend itself. Fear-based violence generally results from trauma, social isolation, or bad interactions with humans or animals. Abused or mistreated dogs or those not exposed to different contexts during their formative months may develop a dread of new situations and respond violently as a protection.

Aggression also stems from frustration. A frustrated dog, whether restrained, denied, or overstimulated, can attack. Dogs on leashes often feel like they can't reach what they want, like another dog or a good fragrance. The dog becomes frustrated and aggressive when it feels powerless.

Territory is another typical hostility factor. Dogs are territorial and may attack if they feel invaded. When strangers approach their home, yard, or favorite area, this can happen. Territorial aggression is typical in breeds that were bred to guard property, but any dog that feels threatened might develop it.

Aggression is also driven by defense. Dogs may attack to defend themselves or their owners. Dogs that are particularly attached to their owners and feel the need to defend them from nonexistent threats often exhibit this form of aggression.

Remember that genetics, environment, and taught behavior shape a dog's hostility. Breeds bred for guarding, herding, or protection may be more reactive or aggressive in specific situations. Rarely is genetics the only factor. The way a dog is raised, socialized, and trained affects its behavior. A dog that was not properly socialized with other animals or humans as a puppy may be afraid or reactive as an adult. If canines were accidentally rewarded for aggression, they can learn it.

## Safety Matters

Managers of violent dogs must always ensure safety for the dog, the owner, and anybody else who may come into touch with the dog. Without proper management, aggressive dogs can cause scratches, bites, and other injuries. Every dog owner must take precautions to keep their pet safe.

Biting is a major risk of aggressive dogs. Dog bites can range from minor nips to catastrophic wounds, depending on size, strength, and conditions. Bites can cause physical and emotional harm to victims, so owners should be concerned. This is especially true for bitten children. In many places, dogs who bite can be designated "dangerous" or euthanized, which might have legal ramifications for the owner.

Because of these concerns, this book emphasizes safety. Managing an aggressive dog involves modifying its behavior and keeping everyone safe during training. Leashes, harnesses, muzzles, and gates are used to physically restrain the dog while it learns better behavior. These technologies establish a controlled setting where the dog can learn without endangering others.

When working with an aggressive or reactive dog, reasonable expectations are crucial. Behavior change takes time, so expecting instant results might be discouraging. Depending on the dog's environment, history, and training consistency, improvement can take weeks, months, or years. Owners must be patient and committed, accepting setbacks and gradual development. Even difficult dogs can develop with continuous, positive training.

As a dog owner, you must realize that training an aggressive dog is a shared duty. An violent dog impacts the owner, other pets, family, neighbors, and strangers. In order to protect themselves and the neighborhood, dog owners must take action to correct their pet's behavior.

Owning an aggressive dog is difficult, but it doesn't have to be scary or lonely. Dog owners can reduce aggression and reactivity by being proactive, reinforcing, and prioritizing safety. The procedure is difficult, but a happier, calmer, and safer dog is worth it.

In the following chapters, we'll discuss the origins of aggression, how to change your dog's behavior, and positive reinforcement. Every dog can change, and with the correct tools and devotion, you can teach your dog to be calm in stressful situations.

# Chapter 2

# Understanding Canine Behavior

W hen it comes to training aggressive or reactive dogs, understanding the underlying behavior is key. Dogs, just like humans, experience the world through a mix of sensory inputs and learned behaviors, and they communicate in ways that are often misunderstood by their owners. By grasping how dogs perceive the world and communicate, we can better address behavioral issues and implement effective training.

In this chapter, we will delve into the science behind canine behavior, explore how dogs communicate with body language and vocalizations, and examine how early socialization impacts adult behavior. Along the way, we'll introduce some interesting statistics and facts to provide a clearer picture.

## The Science Behind

## Behavior

Dogs don't see or experience the world in the same way we do. To effectively train them, we need to step into their world—one that's dominated by smell, sound, and body language. Understanding these differences will help us interpret their behaviors more accurately.

## How Dogs Perceive the World

### 1. Sense of Smell

Dogs have an extraordinary sense of smell, which is their primary way of perceiving the world. To put things into perspective:

- Dogs have about 300 million olfactory receptors, compared to our 5 million.

- Their sense of smell is up to **100,000 times more acute** than ours.

- In fact, dogs can detect some odors in parts per trillion, meaning they can differentiate between a wide array of smells that are imperceptible to humans.

This makes scent a central part of how dogs understand their surroundings. When a dog is sniffing during a walk, it's not just being distracted—it's gathering information about the environment, from who passed by recently to what kind of animals are in the area. This reliance on scent also explains why certain behaviors, like marking territory, are instinctual for dogs.

### 2. Sense of Hearing

Dogs are highly attuned to sounds, and they can hear frequencies far beyond what humans can detect:

- A dog's hearing range is approximately **40 to 60 kHz**, while humans hear up to 20 kHz.

- Dogs can hear sounds from four times the distance humans can, making them more sensitive to distant noises like car engines, other animals, or footsteps.

This heightened hearing sensitivity is one reason why some dogs seem startled or reactive to noises that don't bother us. A distant thunderstorm, a neighbor's lawnmower, or even high-pitched sounds from electronic devices may trigger a response in a dog that seems confusing to its human companions.

**3. Vision**

Contrary to popular belief, dogs are not completely colorblind. They see the world in shades of blue and yellow, but they have limited ability to see red or green.

- Dogs are more attuned to movement and can see in dim light much better than humans, thanks to the structure of their eyes.

- While dogs' vision is not as sharp as humans in terms of detail, they compensate with their enhanced abilities in other senses, especially smell and hearing.

## Canine Communication Signals

Dogs communicate through a combination of body language, facial expressions, vocalizations, and behaviors. Learning how to "read" your dog's signals is vital to understanding their mood and intentions.

1. **Body Language**

The way a dog carries its body can tell you a lot about its emotional state:

- **Tail position**: A high, stiff tail can indicate confidence or aggression, while a tucked tail suggests fear or submission.

- **Ears**: Forward-pointing ears often signal alertness, while flattened ears can indicate fear or discomfort.

- **Posture**: A dog standing tall and stiff may be trying to assert dominance or is feeling defensive. In contrast, a dog lowering its body or rolling over is showing submission.

2. **Facial Expressions**

While dogs don't smile in the same way humans do, they still have a variety of facial expressions that can signal their feelings:

- **Mouth**: A relaxed, slightly open mouth with the tongue hanging out typically shows contentment, while a tight, closed mouth may indicate discomfort or anxiety.

- **Eyes**: Direct eye contact can be a sign of confidence, while looking away or avoiding eye contact is often a sign of submission.

### 3. Vocalizations

Dogs use a range of vocalizations to communicate with humans and other animals:

- **Barking:** Different barks have different meanings. For example, a rapid, continuous bark could mean the dog is excited or alert, while a slow, low bark may indicate frustration or warning.

- **Growling:** Growling is typically a warning sign that a dog feels threatened or is protecting something valuable.

- **Whining:** This often indicates anxiety or a desire for attention, but it can also be a sign of pain or discomfort.

## Normal and Problematic Behavior Differences

Dogs, like humans, exhibit a wide range of behaviors, many of which are completely normal. However, what's considered normal can depend on the breed, individual temperament, and upbringing of the dog. Here's how to differentiate between normal and problematic behaviors:

### 1. Normal Behavior

- **Chewing**: Chewing is a natural behavior for dogs, particularly puppies. It helps them explore their environment and alleviate discomfort during teething. However, this behavior can become problematic if the dog starts chewing on inappropriate objects like furniture or shoes.

- **Digging**: Some breeds, like terriers, are more prone to digging because they were originally bred to hunt underground animals. While digging is a normal activity, it becomes problematic when it leads to destruction of property.

- **Barking**: Dogs bark to communicate, but excessive barking, especially without a clear trigger, can be a sign of underlying issues such as anxiety or boredom.

### 2. Problematic Behavior

Problematic behaviors often arise from stress, fear, anxiety, or improper training. Some key examples include:

- **Aggression**: Aggression, whether toward other animals or humans, is always considered problematic. It can stem from fear, dominance, or territorial instincts.

- **Separation anxiety**: Dogs that experience extreme distress when left alone may exhibit destructive behaviors like chewing, digging, or even attempting to escape.

## The Role of Early Socialization

Early socialization is a critical component in shaping a dog's adult behavior. Puppies that are properly socialized are more likely to grow into well-adjusted, confident adult dogs. Let's break down how socialization impacts dogs and why it's so important.

## How Socialization Influences Adult Behavior

The first few months of a puppy's life, particularly between 3 and 14 weeks, are known as the **socialization period**. During this time, puppies are especially receptive to new experiences and stimuli. Positive exposure to different people, animals, environments, and situations during this period can prevent fear-based behaviors, aggression, and anxiety in adulthood.

- **Well-Socialized Puppies**

Puppies exposed to a variety of environments, noises, people, and other animals during their socialization period are more likely to:

- Show confidence in new situations.

- Behave appropriately around other dogs and people.

- Exhibit fewer fear-based behaviors.

- **Poorly Socialized Puppies**

Puppies that miss out on proper socialization may grow into adults that struggle with:

- **Fear-based aggression**: Dogs that haven't been exposed to other animals or humans might react aggressively out of fear when they encounter them later in life.

- **Reactivity**: A lack of exposure to common stimuli, such as cars, children, or other dogs, can lead to heightened reactivity, where a dog overreacts to certain triggers.

## Aggression Impact of Poor Socialization

Dogs that have not been adequately socialized during their formative months are at higher risk of developing aggressive behaviors. This can happen for several reasons:

1. **Fear-Based Aggression**

Lack of socialization can cause a dog to react aggressively out of fear when confronted with unfamiliar situations, people, or animals. In these cases, the dog views these encounters as threats, even when there is no real danger.

**2. Territorial Aggression**

Dogs that have not been exposed to different environments or people may become overly territorial. This often manifests as aggressive behavior when strangers approach their home or personal space.

**3. Leash Reactivity**

Inadequate socialization can also contribute to leash reactivity, where a dog becomes overly aggressive or anxious when encountering other dogs or stimuli while on a leash. Leash reactivity often stems from frustration or fear, particularly if the dog feels trapped or unable to escape the situation.

## Key Statistics on Dog Behavior and Socialization

To further understand the importance of behavior and socialization, let's consider a few statistics:

- According to the **American Veterinary Society of Animal Behavior**, 50% of dog aggression cases reported involve fear-based aggression.

- **The ASPCA** reports that nearly 37% of dogs in shelters exhibit some form of behavioral issue, much of which stems from improper socialization.

- Well-socialized puppies are up to **60% less likely** to develop reactivity or aggression later in life compared to those who miss out on crucial socialization.

Conception of how dogs perceive the world, their methods of communication, and the role early socialization plays in their development is essential for any dog owner.

Armed with this knowledge, you're better equipped to identify normal versus problematic behaviors and take the necessary steps to address them. Early socialization, positive reinforcement, and consistent training will help ensure that your dog grows into a well-adjusted, confident companion.

## Tendencies in Aggression and Reactivity

One of the most fascinating aspects of canine behavior is how much a dog's breed can influence its tendencies toward aggression and reactivity. While every dog is an individual with its own personality and quirks, certain breeds are more predisposed to particular behaviors due to their genetics and historical roles. Understanding these breed-specific traits can help dog owners, trainers, and behaviorists anticipate and address potential problems more effectively.

In this chapter, we will explore how breed traits contribute to reactive and aggressive behaviors. We'll look at examples of breeds that are more prone to these tendencies and discuss how their history, genetics, and purpose influence their behavior. It's important to remember that while breed tendencies play a role, training, socialization, and the individual dog's environment are equally significant factors.

## How Breed Traits Can Contribute to Reactive or Aggressive Behavior

Dogs have been selectively bred for thousands of years to perform specific jobs. Whether herding, hunting, guarding, or companionship, these roles have shaped not only a dog's physical attributes but also its temperament and behavior. As a result, some breeds are more inclined toward certain behaviors, including reactivity and aggression. This doesn't mean that these dogs are "bad" or impossible to manage. Instead, it highlights the importance of understanding the breed's natural tendencies and working with them.

1. **Guarding and Territorial Instincts**

Many breeds have been bred to protect property, livestock, or people. These breeds often have a strong territorial instinct, which can sometimes manifest as aggression or reactivity when they feel their space is being invaded.

- **Breeds with Guarding Instincts**: German Shepherds, Rottweilers, and Doberman Pinschers are just a few examples of breeds bred to guard. Their natural inclination to protect their territory can lead to aggressive behaviors toward strangers or other animals if not properly managed.

- **Reactive Behaviors**: These dogs may bark, growl, or lunge at people or animals they perceive as threats. While this behavior can be desirable in a working dog or guard dog, it becomes problematic when the dog reacts aggressively in situations where there is no real danger, such as when someone visits the home.

## 2. Herding Instincts

Herding breeds, such as Border Collies, Australian Shepherds, and Corgis, are known for their intelligence, energy, and drive to control the movement of other animals. While these traits make them excellent working dogs, they can also lead to reactivity, especially when these dogs try to "herd" other dogs, children, or even adults.

- **Reactivity in Herding Breeds**: The high energy and alertness of herding breeds mean that they are constantly scanning their environment, looking for something to control or manage. This can lead to reactivity, where the dog overreacts to stimuli such as running children, cyclists, or other dogs. They may bark, nip, or chase in an attempt to manage what they see as unruly behavior.

## 3. Predatory Drive

Many breeds were developed to hunt and track animals, and as a result, they have a strong predatory drive. This drive can sometimes be misinterpreted as aggression, especially when the dog is chasing after smaller animals or even children. Breeds such as Greyhounds, Jack Russell Terriers, and Siberian Huskies have strong prey drives that can make them reactive in environments where they encounter smaller animals.

- **Aggression vs. Prey Drive**: It's important to differentiate between aggression and prey drive. When a dog is chasing a smaller animal, it is often acting on instinct rather than aggression. However, this behavior can be dangerous if the dog is not well-trained or if it is unable to distinguish between appropriate and inappropriate targets.

### 4. Fear-Based Reactivity

Some breeds are more prone to fear-based aggression or reactivity due to their sensitive nature or nervous disposition. Breeds like the Chihuahua, Italian Greyhound, or Shih Tzu can be more prone to react aggressively when they feel threatened or anxious, especially if they are not properly socialized.

- **Why Fear-Based Reactivity Occurs**: These smaller or more sensitive breeds may react aggressively as a defense mechanism when they feel they are in danger. In these cases, the aggression is not driven by dominance or territoriality but by fear.

## Examples of Breeds

While any dog can exhibit aggression or reactivity based on its individual experiences, certain breeds are statistically more likely to show these tendencies due to their genetics and historical roles. Let's take a closer look at some breeds that are more prone to specific types of aggressive behavior and what this means for owners and trainers.

## 1. Territorial Aggression: German Shepherd

German Shepherds are known for their intelligence, loyalty, and strong work ethic. They are one of the most popular breeds for police, military, and protection work, thanks to their guarding instincts and courage. However, these same traits can lead to territorial aggression if not properly managed. German Shepherds are naturally protective of their home and family, and they may view unfamiliar people or animals as threats.

- **Behavioral Tendencies**: German Shepherds may bark, growl, or lunge at strangers who come too close to their home or family members. They may also exhibit guarding behaviors over resources such as food or toys.

- **Managing Aggression**: Early socialization and training are critical for managing a German Shepherd's protective instincts. Teaching the dog to differentiate between real threats and everyday situations can help reduce territorial aggression. Positive reinforcement training and controlled exposure to new people and environments are key to ensuring that a German Shepherd learns appropriate responses to strangers.

## 2. Reactivity to Movement: Border Collie

Border Collies are widely regarded as one of the most intelligent dog breeds, and they excel in tasks that require problem-solving, focus, and agility. Originally bred for herding sheep, Border Collies have an intense drive to control movement. This instinct can sometimes lead to reactivity, particularly when the dog is exposed to fast-moving stimuli such as cyclists, joggers, or cars.

- **Behavioral Tendencies**: Border Collies may become fixated on moving objects and attempt to "herd" them. This can involve chasing, barking, and even nipping. While this behavior is a result of the breed's herding instincts, it can be problematic in everyday settings, such as during walks or at the park.

- **Managing Reactivity**: Border Collies need ample mental and physical stimulation to channel their energy and herding instincts in productive ways. Activities such as agility training, puzzle toys, and structured play can help reduce reactivity. It's also essential to teach impulse control and recall commands to manage the dog's response to movement.

## 3. Prey Drive Aggression: Siberian Husky

Siberian Huskies are a breed known for their independence, strength, and high energy levels. Originally bred to pull sleds over long distances, Huskies have a strong prey drive and can be highly reactive to smaller animals. This prey drive can sometimes be mistaken for aggression, especially when a Husky is chasing small animals like squirrels, cats, or even small dogs.

- **Behavioral Tendencies**: Siberian Huskies may become highly excited or focused when they spot small animals, and their natural instinct is to chase. In some cases, they may become aggressive if they catch the animal or if their prey drive is not redirected.

- **Managing Prey Drive**: Huskies benefit from training that focuses on impulse control and redirecting their prey drive. Using commands such as "leave it" or "come" can help prevent unwanted chasing. Additionally, ensuring that Huskies have plenty of physical exercise and opportunities to use their natural instincts in a controlled environment, such as dog sports or games, can help reduce the likelihood of prey-driven aggression.

## 4. Resource Guarding: Rottweiler

Rottweilers are strong, confident dogs with a long history of being used for guarding and protection work. They are loyal and protective of their families, but they can also develop aggressive behaviors related to resource guarding. This can include guarding food, toys, or even their owners.

- **Behavioral Tendencies**: Rottweilers may growl, snap, or bite if they feel that someone is trying to take away something they value. This behavior is often rooted in their natural guarding instincts but can become problematic if it is not addressed early on.

- **Managing Resource Guarding**: Preventing and managing resource guarding in Rottweilers requires early socialization and training. Teaching the dog to "trade" items or to respond to commands like "drop it" can help reduce possessive behaviors. It's also important to teach the dog that relinquishing an item will lead to a positive outcome, such as receiving a treat or praise.

## 5. Fear-Based Aggression: Chihuahua

Chihuahuas, despite their small size, are known for having bold and sometimes feisty personalities. Due to their diminutive stature, Chihuahuas can feel threatened by larger animals or unfamiliar people, leading to fear-based aggression. This type of aggression is often seen in small breeds, as they are more vulnerable and may feel the need to defend themselves when they perceive a threat.

- **Behavioral Tendencies**: A Chihuahua may bark, growl, or snap at people or animals that get too close. This behavior is usually a result of fear rather than true aggression, but it can still lead to problematic interactions if not managed.

- **Managing Fear-Based Aggression**: Building confidence through positive reinforcement training and gradual exposure to new experiences can help reduce fear-based aggression in Chihuahuas. Providing the dog with a safe space and allowing it to approach new situations at its own pace is important for managing this type of aggression.

## Key Statistics on Breed-Specific Aggression

Let's take a look at some statistics to highlight the role that breed tendencies can play in aggression:

- A study published by the **American Veterinary Medical Association** found that 20% of reported dog bites in the U.S. come from guard breeds, such as Rottweilers and German Shepherds.

- According to research from **The Journal of Veterinary Behavior**, breeds with strong prey drives, such as Siberian Huskies and Greyhounds, are twice as likely to show aggressive behaviors toward smaller animals.

- **The American Temperament Test Society** reports that herding breeds like Border Collies have a pass rate of over 80% in temperament tests, but they are more likely to display reactivity when exposed to moving objects.

While breed traits play a significant role in shaping a dog's behavior, it's important to remember that every dog is an individual. Genetics, upbringing, training, and environment all contribute to how a dog behaves.

Understanding your dog's breed-specific tendencies allows you to anticipate potential behavioral challenges and address them through proper training and socialization.

By working with your dog's natural instincts rather than against them, you can create a more harmonious and manageable relationship.

# Chapter 3

# Identifying Aggression and Reactivity

Aggression and reactivity in dogs can stem from a variety of causes, and understanding these behaviors is the first step toward managing them. Often misunderstood, aggressive and reactive behaviors are not always signs of a "bad" dog. Instead, they frequently signal underlying emotions such as fear, frustration, or a desire to protect. In this chapter, we will explore the different types of aggression, what triggers reactive behaviors, and how to differentiate between aggression and fear-based reactivity.

## Types of Aggression

Aggression in dogs manifests in different ways, and understanding the type of aggression your dog exhibits is crucial for determining the appropriate training and behavior modification techniques. Below are five common types of aggression seen in dogs:

### 1. Fear-Based Aggression

Fear-based aggression is one of the most common forms of aggression in dogs. It occurs when a dog feels threatened or cornered and reacts aggressively to protect itself. Dogs that exhibit fear-based aggression may not inherently want to harm anyone but feel they have no other choice in a given situation.

- **Signs of Fear-Based Aggression**: Dogs displaying this type of aggression often have specific body language cues that show fear before they become aggressive. These can include:

  - Cowering or backing away.

  - Flattening their ears.

  - Tucking their tail between their legs.

  - Avoiding eye contact.

  - Growling or snapping if the threat continues.

- **Common Triggers**: Fear-based aggression is usually triggered by situations in which the dog feels unsafe or threatened. Some common triggers include:

  - Encounters with unfamiliar people or dogs.

  - Sudden movements or loud noises.

  - Being cornered or restrained.

  - Past traumatic experiences, such as abuse or neglect.

- **Case Example**: A rescue dog that was mistreated in its past home might become aggressive when approached by a stranger. The dog's aggression stems from the fear of being harmed again, not from a desire to attack.

Fear-based aggression can often be managed through desensitization and counter-conditioning. By gradually exposing the dog to its triggers in a controlled environment and pairing those exposures with positive reinforcement, the dog can learn to feel safe and reduce its aggressive responses.

## 2. Territorial Aggression

Territorial aggression occurs when a dog feels the need to defend its space or possessions. This behavior is rooted in a dog's instinct to protect its home, yard, or even its family members. While territorial aggression can be useful for guard dogs, it becomes problematic when the dog cannot differentiate between real threats and harmless situations.

- **Signs of Territorial Aggression**: Dogs showing territorial aggression may exhibit:

  - Intense barking when someone approaches their home or yard.

  - Growling, snarling, or lunging at perceived intruders.

  - Pacing or standing in a defensive posture.

  - Stiff body language and direct eye contact.

- **Common Triggers**: Territorial aggression is typically triggered by:

  - People or animals entering the dog's home or property.

  - Someone approaching the dog's belongings, such as toys, food, or bedding.

  - Visitors coming into the house, especially if the dog has not been properly socialized with strangers.

- **Case Example**: A Rottweiler that has been trained as a guard dog may become aggressive when a delivery person comes to the door. While this behavior might seem appropriate in some contexts, it can become problematic if the dog reacts aggressively to every visitor.

To manage territorial aggression, it's important to set clear boundaries for the dog. Training the dog to associate visitors with positive experiences, such as receiving treats when someone enters the home, can help reduce territorial aggression. Additionally, ensuring that the dog has a designated space where it feels safe and does not feel the need to defend can also help manage this behavior.

## 3. Resource Guarding

Resource guarding is a type of aggression where a dog becomes possessive over objects, food, or even people. This behavior is natural in many animals, as they instinctively want to protect valuable resources. However, in domestic dogs, this behavior can lead to aggression if not managed properly.

- **Signs of Resource Guarding**: A dog that is resource guarding may:

  - Growl, snap, or bite when someone approaches their food bowl, toys, or other possessions.

  - Stiffen its body and hover over the resource.

  - Show aggressive behaviors when other pets or people get close to the person they are "protecting."

- **Common Triggers**: The most common triggers for resource guarding include:

  - Approaching the dog while it is eating or drinking.

  - Trying to take away a toy or bone.

  - Petting or touching a dog that is guarding a person, such as their owner or another family member.

- **Case Example**: A Labrador Retriever might growl when someone tries to take away its favorite chew toy. If the dog perceives a threat to its resource, it will escalate its aggression to protect it.

Resource guarding can be managed by teaching the dog that sharing its resources leads to positive outcomes. Techniques such as trading, where the dog is given a high-value treat in exchange for relinquishing the resource, can help reduce the dog's need to guard.

## 4. Redirected Aggression

Redirected aggression occurs when a dog becomes agitated or frustrated by something it cannot reach or control, and then redirects its aggression toward a nearby person, animal, or object. This type of aggression is often impulsive and can be surprising for both the dog and the target.

- **Signs of Redirected Aggression**: This type of aggression typically occurs when a dog is in an agitated state, such as when it:

  - Becomes frustrated by seeing another dog it cannot reach while on a leash.

  - Experiences stress from a loud noise or commotion.

  - Engages in a high-energy play session that escalates too quickly.

- **Common Triggers**: Redirected aggression is often triggered by:

  - Barriers preventing the dog from reaching its target, such as being on a leash or behind a fence.

  - Overstimulation during play or social interactions.

  - The dog being in a heightened state of arousal due to environmental factors like loud noises, crowds, or other dogs.

- **Case Example**: A dog on a leash may become agitated when it sees another dog across the street. Unable to reach the dog, it may suddenly turn and bite its owner out of frustration.

To manage redirected aggression, it's important to recognize when the dog is becoming overly aroused and remove it from the situation before the aggression escalates. Teaching impulse control and using calming techniques, such as redirecting the dog's focus to a treat or toy, can help prevent redirected aggression.

## 5. Predatory Aggression

Predatory aggression is driven by a dog's natural instinct to chase and capture prey. This type of aggression is not usually accompanied by the typical warning signs, such as growling or barking, because it is part of a deeply ingrained hunting behavior. Predatory aggression is often seen in dogs with high prey drive, such as sighthounds, terriers, and certain working breeds.

- **Signs of Predatory Aggression**: This type of aggression often manifests as:

  - Intense focus on a moving object, such as a squirrel, rabbit, or even a running child.

  - Chasing, stalking, or attempting to capture the target.

  - Silent, swift movements as the dog engages its prey drive.

- **Common Triggers**: Predatory aggression is typically triggered by:

  - Fast-moving objects, such as bicycles, cars, or animals.

  - Small animals that resemble prey, such as rabbits, squirrels, or birds.

  - Children running or playing, which can trigger a dog's instinct to chase.

- **Case Example**: A Greyhound may chase after a small animal it spots during a walk. Without proper recall training, the dog may catch and harm the animal due to its predatory instincts.

Managing predatory aggression requires careful control of the dog's environment and the use of distraction techniques. Training the dog to respond to recall commands and redirecting its focus to a toy or treat can help mitigate the dog's natural prey drive.

## Understanding Reactivity

Reactivity in dogs is often confused with aggression, but the two are not the same. Reactivity refers to a heightened response to stimuli, which may or may not involve aggression. Reactive dogs may bark, lunge, or become overly excited when confronted with certain triggers, such as other dogs, loud noises, or strangers. Unlike aggression, reactivity is not always driven by a desire to cause harm.

## What Triggers Reactive Behavior?

Reactive behavior in dogs can be triggered by a variety of factors, including environmental stimuli, unfamiliar people or animals, and past experiences. Common triggers for reactivity include:

- **Strangers**: Some dogs are reactive to unfamiliar people, especially if they have not been properly socialized. This reactivity can manifest as barking, lunging, or growling when a stranger approaches.

- **Other Dogs**: Dogs that have not been well-socialized with other dogs may react strongly when they encounter another dog. This reactivity may include barking, pulling on the leash, or even aggression in some cases.

- **Loud Noises**: Sudden, loud noises, such as fireworks, thunderstorms, or construction sounds, can trigger reactivity in noise-sensitive dogs. This reactivity often takes the form of barking, pacing, or hiding.

- **New Environments**: Some dogs become reactive when they are taken to new places, such as parks, pet stores, or busy city streets. The unfamiliar sights, sounds, and smells can overwhelm the dog and trigger a reactive response.

## The Difference Between Aggression and Fear-Based Reactivity

It's essential to understand the distinction between aggression and fear-based reactivity, as the two are often confused. While aggression is typically associated with a dog's intent to cause harm, fear-based reactivity stems from a heightened emotional response to perceived threats or stimuli. A reactive dog may not want to harm anyone but instead feels overwhelmed or frightened by the situation, leading to defensive behaviors.

- **Aggression**: Aggression is characterized by offensive actions that are meant to intimidate or harm another person, dog, or animal. Dogs that are aggressive will often exhibit a combination of warning signs (growling, snarling, or snapping) and actions (lunging, biting) with the intent of defending themselves or asserting dominance.

- **Fear-Based Reactivity**: In contrast, fear-based reactivity occurs when a dog feels threatened or insecure and reacts by trying to scare off the perceived threat. The key difference here is the dog's motivation: a reactive dog is trying to protect itself and avoid confrontation, while an aggressive dog may be looking to assert control or dominance over the situation.

- **Body Language Differences**:

  ○ **Aggressive Dogs**: Typically, an aggressive dog will exhibit stiff, confident body language with a forward stance, raised hackles, and direct eye contact. The tail may be held high, and the dog might growl or bark with a deep tone.

○ **Reactive Dogs**: A reactive dog, on the other hand, may display signs of fear or anxiety before escalating into reactivity. These can include crouching, tucking the tail, or flattening the ears. The dog may bark or lunge but in a more erratic or desperate manner, trying to create space between itself and the perceived threat.

## Case Study: Fear-Based Reactivity vs. Aggression

To illustrate the difference between aggression and fear-based reactivity, consider two dogs in similar situations:

1. **Dog A: Aggressive**

Dog A is a territorial breed, such as a German Shepherd, who has not been properly socialized with other dogs. During a walk, it sees another dog approaching and immediately stiffens its body, raises its hackles, and growls. As the other dog gets closer, Dog A lunges and tries to bite, with the clear intent of asserting control over the situation and protecting its space.

1. **Dog B: Fear-Based Reactivity**

Dog B is a rescue dog who was not socialized as a puppy and is easily startled by new dogs and people. When another dog approaches on a walk, Dog B starts by cowering, backing away, and showing signs of fear (flattened ears, tail tucked). However, as the other dog comes closer, Dog B begins barking frantically and lunges in an attempt to create distance. Dog B's behavior is driven by fear and a desire to avoid confrontation, not to dominate or harm the other dog.

Both dogs exhibit similar outward behaviors—lunging, barking, and aggressive posturing—but the underlying causes and motivations are entirely different. Recognizing this difference is crucial for choosing the right training approach.

## Managing Aggression and Reactivity

Understanding whether a dog's behavior is driven by aggression or fear-based reactivity is key to implementing the right behavior modification strategies. For aggressive dogs, training may focus on impulse control, setting boundaries, and teaching alternative behaviors. For reactive dogs, desensitization and counter-conditioning are essential to help them feel more comfortable and confident in stressful situations.

**Key Strategies for Managing Aggression:**

1. **Impulse Control**: Teaching dogs to wait, focus, and control their reactions before escalating into aggressive behavior.

2. **Clear Boundaries**: Setting clear rules and expectations, such as not guarding resources or reacting to every visitor at the door.

3. **Replacement Behaviors**: Training the dog to perform alternative, positive behaviors in situations where aggression might occur.

**Key Strategies for Managing Reactivity:**

1. **Desensitization**: Gradually exposing the dog to its triggers in a controlled environment, starting with low-intensity situations and building up over time.

2. **Counter-Conditioning**: Changing the dog's emotional response to its triggers by pairing the exposure with positive reinforcement (e.g., treats, praise).

3. **Safe Spaces**: Providing a safe space for the dog to retreat to when it feels overwhelmed, reducing the chance of reactive behavior.

Understanding the types of aggression and reactivity in dogs is essential for any owner or trainer. Aggression and reactivity may look similar on the surface, but they often stem from different emotional states, such as fear, frustration, or territorial instincts. Identifying the underlying cause of a dog's behavior is the first step in developing a tailored plan to manage and reduce these behaviors.

## Case Studies:

### Real-Life Examples of Aggressive and Reactive Dogs

When it comes to understanding and managing aggressive or reactive dogs, real-life examples can provide valuable insights. Each dog is unique, but the patterns and triggers that lead to aggressive or reactive behavior often follow common themes. By examining case studies, we can explore how different types of aggression manifest in individual dogs and how these behaviors can be successfully managed with the right approach.

In this section, we'll look at several real-life examples of aggressive and reactive dogs, focusing on their specific triggers, the underlying causes of their behaviors, and the methods used to address and improve these behaviors.

## Case Study 1:

### Max – Fear-Based Aggression Triggered by Strangers

## Background:

Max, a five-year-old mixed-breed dog, was adopted from a local shelter when he was just a year old. He had spent the first year of his life with little human interaction, living mostly in isolation. When he arrived at the shelter, Max showed signs of extreme fear, particularly around men. His new owners were kind and patient, but they quickly noticed that Max would become aggressive whenever strangers entered the house or approached him on walks.

## Behavior:

Max's aggression manifested through growling, barking, and lunging at strangers. When guests came to the house, he would bark incessantly and retreat to a corner, only to lash out if someone approached too quickly. His body language included cowering, flattened ears, and a tucked tail—all classic signs of fear. Despite his outward aggression, Max's behavior was driven entirely by fear and a desire to protect himself from perceived threats.

## Triggers:

Max's primary triggers included:

- **Strangers entering the home**: Whenever someone new came into the house, Max would immediately become agitated and defensive.

- **Men**: He showed a particularly strong reaction to men, likely due to negative past experiences with a male figure before he was rescued.

- **Unexpected approaches**: Max became aggressive if anyone, even familiar people, approached him too quickly, particularly if they reached out to pet him.

## Behavior Modification Plan:

Max's owners worked with a professional dog trainer who specialized in fear-based aggression. The plan focused on:

1. **Desensitization and Counter-Conditioning**: Max was slowly introduced to new people in a controlled environment, beginning with short, non-threatening encounters. Strangers would toss treats from a distance, helping Max associate their presence with positive outcomes rather than fear.

2. **Safe Space**: Max's owners created a safe space for him in the house—a quiet corner where he could retreat when guests arrived. This helped reduce his anxiety by giving him control over his environment.

3. **Gradual Exposure**: Instead of forcing Max into uncomfortable situa-

tions, his owners gradually increased his exposure to strangers. Guests were instructed not to approach him or make direct eye contact, allowing Max to decide when he felt comfortable enough to interact.

## Results:

Over several months, Max's fear-based aggression significantly improved. While he still showed some caution around new people, particularly men, he no longer barked incessantly or lashed out when guests entered the house. Max learned to associate strangers with positive experiences, thanks to the gradual exposure and the use of treats as rewards. By building trust and confidence, Max's aggressive reactions were minimized, and his overall quality of life improved.

## Case Study 2:

### Bella – Territorial Aggression in a Family Home

## Background:

Bella, a three-year-old Rottweiler, was raised in a loving family home. She had been well-socialized as a puppy and had always been friendly with her family members. However, as she grew older, Bella developed strong territorial instincts. She became protective of her home and yard, barking aggressively whenever someone approached the house. Bella's family grew concerned when she began lunging at delivery workers and even showing signs of aggression toward visitors she had met before.

## Behavior:

Bella's territorial aggression manifested in several ways:
- **Barking at anyone near the house**: Bella would bark aggressively if

someone even walked past the front yard, and the behavior intensified when someone knocked on the door.

- **Guarding the yard**: When outside, Bella would patrol the perimeter of the yard, barking and lunging at anyone she perceived as an intruder.

- **Aggression toward visitors**: Once visitors entered the house, Bella would sometimes growl or act defensively, especially if they moved too quickly or approached her family members.

## Triggers:

Bella's triggers were primarily related to perceived threats to her territory, including:

- **Strangers near or entering the home**: Bella's aggression was strongest when people she didn't recognize approached the house.

- **Delivery workers**: The sight of delivery trucks and workers approaching the front door would set Bella off, leading to intense barking and lunging.

- **Visitors interacting with family members**: Bella sometimes reacted aggressively when visitors made physical contact with her family members, such as hugging or shaking hands.

## Behavior Modification Plan:

To address Bella's territorial aggression, her family worked with a behaviorist to implement the following strategies:

1. **Boundary Training**: Bella was taught specific boundaries around the house and yard, including where she was allowed to be when visitors arrived. This training included teaching her to stay in a designated area

when the doorbell rang, rather than rushing to the door.

2. **Positive Reinforcement for Calm Behavior**: Bella was rewarded with treats and praise when she remained calm in the presence of visitors or delivery workers. The goal was to teach her that visitors were not a threat and that calm behavior resulted in positive outcomes.

3. **Controlled Greetings**: Bella's family practiced controlled greetings with visitors. Guests were instructed to ignore Bella when they first arrived, allowing her to calm down before any interaction occurred. Once she was calm, she was allowed to approach on her terms, and only then was she rewarded with treats or attention.

## Results:

Over time, Bella's territorial aggression diminished. She became more relaxed when people approached the house and learned to remain calm when the doorbell rang. By setting clear boundaries and using positive reinforcement, Bella's family was able to manage her territorial instincts while ensuring she felt secure in her role as a protector.

## Case Study 3:

### Duke – Resource Guarding Over Food and Toys

## Background:

Duke, a two-year-old Labrador Retriever, had always been a friendly and playful dog. However, as he grew older, he developed a habit of guarding his food bowl and toys. Duke would growl and snap if anyone came too close while he was eating or playing with his favorite toys. This behavior caused concern for his owners, particularly when Duke's resource guarding extended to interactions with their children.

## Behavior:

Duke's resource guarding was specific to items he valued highly:

- **Food guarding**: Duke would growl and snap if anyone approached his food bowl while he was eating. He became particularly aggressive if someone tried to take food away or move his bowl.

- **Toy guarding**: Duke showed similar behavior with his favorite toys. If anyone tried to take a toy from him, he would react defensively, sometimes lunging or snapping.

- **Protectiveness over high-value items**: Duke was especially protective of bones or treats, often retreating to a corner to guard them and becoming aggressive if someone tried to approach.

## Triggers:

Duke's aggression was triggered primarily by:

- **Approaching him during meals**: Even standing near Duke while he was eating would provoke growling and defensive behavior.

- **Taking toys or treats away**: Attempting to take a toy or bone from Duke, even in a playful context, led to aggressive responses.

- **Children getting too close**: Duke became especially protective of his food and toys when the family's young children were near, making his resource guarding a serious safety concern.

## Behavior Modification Plan:

To manage Duke's resource guarding, his family implemented a structured training plan with the help of a professional:

1. **Trading Game**: Duke was taught the "trade" game, where he learned to exchange his toys or food for high-value treats. This helped him understand that giving up an item would result in a positive reward, rather than a loss.

2. **Desensitization to Approaching People**: The family worked on desensitizing Duke to people approaching while he was eating or playing. At first, they would approach at a distance and toss treats toward him, gradually moving closer as Duke became more comfortable.

3. **Teaching "Leave It" Command**: Duke was trained to respond to the "leave it" command, teaching him to relinquish items on cue. This command helped manage his resource guarding behavior by giving his owners control over potentially aggressive situations.

## Results:

After consistent training, Duke's resource-guarding behavior significantly improved. He learned to trade his toys and food for treats, reducing his defensiveness around valuable items. Duke's owners also noticed that he became less anxious when people were near his food bowl, and his interactions with the children became safer. While some mild resource guarding remained, it was no longer a significant issue, and Duke's overall behavior improved.

# Chapter 4

# Assessing the Individual Dog

E very dog is different, with its own set of experiences, temperament, and behaviors. This makes it essential for dog owners and trainers to assess each dog individually, rather than relying on assumptions or generalizations about breed or background. In this chapter, we will explore the importance of conducting a thorough behavioral assessment, recognizing patterns and triggers, understanding what causes aggressive or reactive behavior, and working within your dog's behavioral threshold to achieve effective training.

## Behavioral Assessments

A behavioral assessment is a critical first step in understanding a dog's specific challenges and needs. Whether you're dealing with aggression, reactivity, or more general behavioral issues, it's crucial to assess the dog safely and accurately to design a tailored training plan. Behavioral assessments provide insight into the dog's emotional state, how it responds to different stimuli, and what kind of management or modification techniques might be necessary.

### How to Conduct a Safe and Accurate Behavioral Assessment

Conducting a behavioral assessment requires patience, careful observation, and a non-confrontational approach. The goal is to observe the dog's natural reactions to a variety of situations without provoking unnecessary stress or aggression. Here are some key steps to ensure a safe and accurate assessment:

1. **Set the Right Environment**:

The first thing to consider when assessing a dog's behavior is the environment. Choose a quiet, neutral space where the dog feels comfortable. Avoid crowded or overly stimulating areas, as this may trigger reactive behavior unrelated to the dog's usual temperament. This is particularly important for dogs prone to fear-based aggression or overstimulation.

2. **Observe the Dog's Body Language**:

Body language is one of the most important indicators of how a dog is feeling. Subtle signs can reveal a great deal about whether the dog is comfortable, anxious, or on edge. Look for signals such as:

- **Relaxed ears and tail**: Indicates calm and comfort.

- **Tense muscles, raised hackles**: Suggests heightened arousal or aggression.

- **Yawning or licking lips**: Often signs of stress or anxiety.

- **Cowering or tucking the tail**: Indicates fear or submission.

By observing how the dog holds its body and moves in response to different stimuli, you can get an initial sense of its emotional state.

3. **Introduce Gradual Stimuli**:

When assessing how a dog reacts to different situations, it's essential to introduce stimuli slowly and in a controlled manner. For example, if the dog is suspected of being reactive to other dogs, start by observing how it responds to distant, non-threatening dogs. Gradually reduce the distance to see how the dog's behavior changes. Similarly, if the dog is territorial, introduce new people into the environment slowly and watch for signs of tension or discomfort.

**4. Focus on Non-Invasive Techniques**:

Avoid physically handling the dog during the initial assessment unless necessary. The goal is to observe the dog's natural behavior without forcing it into stressful situations. Use a calm voice and neutral body language to avoid escalating any aggressive or reactive tendencies.

**5. Take Notes on Behavior**:

Keeping detailed notes during the assessment is crucial for identifying patterns and triggers later. Record how the dog responds to different stimuli, including sounds, sights, smells, and social interactions. Notes on body language, vocalizations (such as barking or growling), and overall demeanor will help you better understand the dog's behavior in different contexts.

## Recognizing Patterns and Triggers in Your Dog's Behavior

One of the main goals of a behavioral assessment is to identify patterns in the dog's reactions. By doing this, you can start to isolate specific triggers—situations, objects, or interactions that lead to undesirable behavior, such as aggression or reactivity. Here's how to start recognizing these patterns:

1. **Observe Reactions Over Time**:

A single instance of aggression or reactivity may not be enough to establish a pattern. Watch the dog's behavior over several days or weeks, especially in a variety of settings, to see if there are consistent reactions to certain stimuli. For example, does the dog always bark aggressively when approached by strangers? Does it only react this way when on a leash but not when off-leash? These are important distinctions that help pinpoint the behavior's root causes.

1. **Notice Escalation**:

Many dogs give subtle warnings before they escalate into aggression or reactivity. This might include stiffening their posture, growling, or avoiding eye contact. Paying attention to these early signs allows you to intervene before the behavior escalates into something more serious, like biting or lunging.

1. **Identify Emotional States**:

Dogs, like people, experience a range of emotions that influence their behavior. A dog that feels anxious, scared, or overwhelmed will act differently than one that feels calm and confident. Behavioral patterns often reflect a dog's emotional state:

- **Fear**: Dogs that feel fearful may react by freezing, fleeing, or becoming aggressive to protect themselves.

- **Frustration**: If a dog is not getting what it wants (for example, being held back on a leash from approaching another dog), it may become reactive out of frustration.

- **Excitement**: Overly excited dogs may exhibit jumping, barking, or other forms of hyperactive behavior that can escalate into reactivity if not managed.

**4. Behavioral Contexts:**

Some dogs may only display aggression or reactivity in specific situations. For example:

- A dog may be perfectly calm at home but become aggressive at the vet.

- Another dog might play well with familiar dogs but become reactive toward unfamiliar dogs at the park.

Understanding the context in which behaviors occur is key to developing an effective management plan. Not all behavior is generalized across all situations.

# Understanding Triggers

Once you've identified behavioral patterns, the next step is to understand what triggers these behaviors. Triggers are specific stimuli that cause the dog to react aggressively or become highly aroused. Identifying these triggers is critical to managing and modifying the behavior.

## How to Identify Specific Triggers That Lead to Aggression or Reactivity

### 1. **Look for Common Denominators**:

If a dog becomes aggressive or reactive in seemingly unrelated situations, look for the common denominators. For example:

- Does the dog react aggressively to men but not women?

- Does it react only when on a leash or in the backyard, but not when free to roam in a neutral space? These common elements can reveal the dog's underlying fear or discomfort.

### 2. **Note the Timing of the Reaction:**

Sometimes, the timing of a dog's reaction can help pinpoint the trigger. For example, a dog that starts barking aggressively immediately after someone knocks on the door is likely triggered by the sound. Another dog that becomes agitated only when approached closely by another dog may be reacting to proximity.

### 3. **Environmental Factors**:

Environmental triggers play a significant role in how dogs behave. Loud noises (such as thunderstorms, fireworks, or construction sounds), unfamiliar settings (like busy streets or veterinary clinics), or chaotic environments (crowded parks or noisy homes) can all contribute to aggressive or reactive behaviors.

### 4. **Social Triggers**:

Some dogs are sensitive to social dynamics, including interactions with other dogs, people, or even children. For instance:

- A dog may become reactive when other dogs invade its personal space.

- It may show aggression when new people approach its owner, viewing them as a potential threat.

## Why It's Essential to Identify the Underlying Causes Before Starting Training

Knowing the specific triggers that cause aggression or reactivity is essential before implementing a training plan. Training without understanding the root causes can lead to ineffective results or, worse, exacerbate the problem. Here's why identifying triggers is critical:

1. **Targeted Training**:

Once you've identified a dog's triggers, you can tailor the training to address those specific issues. For example:

- A dog that reacts aggressively to other dogs can benefit from controlled exposure to other dogs at a safe distance, rather than general obedience training.

- A dog that is territorial can be trained to manage its response to guests entering the home.

**2. Preventing Overwhelm:**

If a dog is repeatedly exposed to its triggers without any intervention, the behavior may worsen. For example, a dog that is fearful of loud noises may become more reactive if it is constantly exposed to those noises without learning coping mechanisms. Identifying and managing triggers helps ensure that the dog is not overwhelmed during training.

**3. Building Confidence**:

By gradually introducing the dog to its triggers in a controlled environment, you can build the dog's confidence. This helps reduce the likelihood of reactive behavior in the long term, as the dog learns that it can handle stressful situations without resorting to aggression or panic.

## Behavioral Thresholds

A dog's behavioral threshold refers to the point at which a dog can no longer tolerate a stimulus without reacting. Understanding your dog's threshold is critical for successful training. The goal is to work within this threshold to gradually increase the dog's tolerance for stressful stimuli without pushing it into a reactive or aggressive state.

## Defining Your Dog's Threshold for Reactive Behavior

### 1. Recognizing Early Signs:

Before a dog reaches its threshold, it will often display subtle signs of discomfort or stress. These early signs are your cue that the dog is approaching its limit:

- **Increased attention on the trigger**: The dog might fixate on the object or person that is causing stress, often with stiffened body language or intense focus.

- **Panting or pacing**: If the dog starts panting heavily or pacing back and forth, it could be a sign of anxiety.

- **Whining or low growling**: Vocalizations like whining or low growling often indicate that a dog is feeling uncomfortable and may be approaching its behavioral threshold. Paying attention to these early cues helps prevent the situation from escalating to full-blown aggression or reactivity.

### 2. Gauge Distance and Intensity:

A dog's threshold can often be measured by how far away the trigger needs to be for the dog to remain calm. For example:

- A dog may be fine with other dogs at a distance of 50 feet but start to become reactive when another dog is within 20 feet.

- Loud noises might trigger a response when they occur suddenly and nearby but not when they are faint or far away.

Understanding the dog's specific limits in terms of distance, intensity, and proximity to triggers allows for more controlled training. By gradually reducing the distance or increasing exposure in a controlled way, the dog can build tolerance without being overwhelmed.

**3. Emotional Thresholds**:

Behavioral thresholds aren't just about physical proximity; emotional stressors also play a significant role. For example:

- A dog that's already stressed from a busy day or a long walk might have a lower threshold for reacting aggressively to a trigger compared to a well-rested dog.

- Some dogs have higher tolerance for social interactions on certain days or in familiar environments but reach their limit more quickly in unfamiliar or chaotic settings.

## How to Work Within the Threshold to Avoid Triggering Aggression During Training

### 1. Stay Below the Threshold:

The key to working within your dog's threshold is to keep the dog below its breaking point during training. The goal is to expose the dog to its triggers at a level it can handle without becoming reactive or aggressive. If the dog remains calm and composed, it can focus on learning and processing the training.

For example, suppose a dog becomes reactive to other dogs at a distance of 20 feet. In that case, you might start training at 30 feet, where the dog can still notice the other dogs but remains below its threshold. Over time, the distance can be decreased gradually as the dog becomes more comfortable.

**2. Use Positive Reinforcement**:

Positive reinforcement is critical when working within a dog's threshold. Reward the dog for calm behavior when it is exposed to a trigger at a manageable level. This reinforces the idea that calm behavior is the desired response to the trigger.

For instance, if your dog sees another dog in the distance and remains calm, immediately reward with treats or praise. Over time, the dog will associate the presence of the trigger with positive experiences and will be less likely to react aggressively or fearfully.

**3. Gradual Desensitization**:

Desensitization involves slowly exposing the dog to its triggers over time, always staying within the dog's threshold. Gradually, as the dog's comfort level increases, you can reduce the distance, increase the intensity, or extend the exposure time to the trigger.

For example, suppose a dog is reactive to people approaching its food bowl. In that case, you can start by having someone stand several feet away from the bowl while the dog eats, rewarding calm behavior. Gradually, over time, the person can come closer, all while reinforcing the dog to stay calm.

**4. Control the Environment**:

Working within the threshold requires controlling the environment as much as possible to prevent unplanned or overwhelming stimuli. If your dog's threshold for reactivity is low around other dogs, choose quieter walking routes or go out at less busy times to avoid sudden encounters with multiple dogs. By creating a controlled and predictable environment, you can focus on gradual, positive progress without setbacks caused by overstimulation.

## Case Example: Managing a Dog's Behavioral Threshold

Consider Lucy, a two-year-old Australian Shepherd who becomes highly reactive when she sees bicycles. During walks, Lucy would lunge and bark at cyclists passing by, creating a stressful experience for both her and her owner. Her behavioral threshold was reached whenever a cyclist came within 30 feet of her.

- **Step 1**: The first step was determining that Lucy's threshold for calm behavior was around 50 feet. At this distance, Lucy could see the bicycles but remained composed.

- **Step 2**: Lucy's owner started taking her to a local park and positioned her 50 feet away from the bicycle path. Each time a cyclist passed within her threshold, Lucy was rewarded with treats for staying calm. Over time, the distance was reduced, first to 40 feet, then 30 feet, all while reinforcing calm behavior.

- **Step 3**: After several weeks of controlled exposure and positive re-inforcement, Lucy's behavioral threshold had shifted. She could now tolerate bicycles passing as close as 10 feet without reacting aggressively.

By staying within Lucy's threshold and gradually increasing her exposure, her owner was able to help Lucy become more comfortable with bicycles without overwhelming her.

Assessing your dog's behavior is the foundation of any effective training plan. By conducting a thorough behavioral assessment, recognizing patterns and triggers, and understanding your dog's unique threshold for reactive behavior, you can create a targeted approach that addresses the root causes of aggression or reactivity.

Behavioral assessments allow you to observe your dog's natural responses in a controlled environment, helping you understand its emotional state and specific triggers.

Recognizing these triggers is essential for targeted training, ensuring that the dog is not overwhelmed or pushed beyond its limits. Working within your dog's threshold is key to preventing aggression during training, enabling you to build its confidence and tolerance over time.

Ultimately, every dog has the potential to improve, but it requires patience, consistency, and a thorough understanding of its individual needs. With the right approach, even the most reactive or aggressive dogs can learn to navigate the world with greater calm and confidence.

# Chapter 5

# Building a Training Foundation

Training a dog is not just about teaching tricks or commands—it's about building a strong foundation for behavior control, impulse management, and focus. For dogs that struggle with aggression or reactivity, having a solid training foundation is crucial for long-term success.

Without mastering basic obedience, it's challenging to address more complex behavioral issues. In this chapter, we will explore the importance of basic commands, how to build focus and impulse control, and the tools necessary to ensure a safe and productive training process.

## The Importance of Basic Obedience

Basic obedience serves as the cornerstone for all dog training, especially when it comes to managing aggression and reactivity. Commands like "sit," "stay," "recall," and "place" provide structure and help establish communication between you and your dog. With these commands, you can intervene when your dog is about to exhibit undesirable behavior and redirect its focus.

## How Basic Commands Can Be the Foundation for Managing Aggression

1. **Control and Management**:

Basic obedience commands allow you to maintain control over your dog in a variety of situations. When your dog is on the verge of reacting aggressively to a trigger, having solid obedience skills means you can quickly redirect its attention and prevent escalation. For instance:

- **"Sit" and "stay"**: These commands help interrupt aggressive behavior before it starts. Asking a dog to sit and stay when it begins to fixate on a potential trigger gives the dog something else to focus on.

- **"Recall"**: Recall (the "come" command) is vital for pulling your dog out of potentially dangerous situations, such as when it's about to lunge at another dog or chase after something. A dog with a reliable recall will stop what it's doing and return to you, avoiding further conflict.

2. **Building Trust and Confidence:**
Obedience training also helps build trust between you and your dog. When a dog knows what is expected and consistently follows commands, it feels more secure in its environment. This confidence reduces the likelihood of aggressive or reactive behaviors, as the dog no longer feels the need to assert itself in uncertain situations.

3. **Structured Environment**:
Dogs thrive in environments where they understand the rules and boundaries. Basic obedience commands create a structured environment where your dog knows what to expect and how to behave. This structure is particularly important for dogs prone to aggression, as it reduces anxiety and gives them a predictable framework for responding to stimuli.

## Teaching for Behavior Control

Let's break down how teaching these fundamental commands can help manage aggression and reactivity:

1. **"Sit"**:

"Sit" is one of the first commands most dogs learn, and it serves as a simple way to get your dog to focus on you. When a dog is sitting, it's less likely to engage in problematic behaviors such as lunging or jumping. Here's how to use "sit" for behavior control:

- **Training Tip**: Start by asking your dog to sit whenever it encounters a potential trigger (like another dog or a stranger). This interrupts the fixation and provides an opportunity for the dog to focus on you instead of the trigger.

- **Practical Example**: If your dog tends to jump on visitors, teaching it to sit when people arrive gives the dog a clear alternative to jumping.

### 2. "Stay":

"Stay" is essential for preventing your dog from charging at a person, dog, or object that might provoke aggressive behavior. A well-taught "stay" command allows you to control your dog's movements and ensure it remains calm.

- **Training Tip**: Start with short "stay" sessions in a distraction-free environment and gradually increase the duration and difficulty by adding distractions like other dogs or people walking by.

- **Practical Example**: When your dog sees another dog in the distance and begins to show signs of reactivity, asking for a "stay" command can prevent the dog from moving toward the trigger, keeping it calm and controlled.

### 3. "Recall" (Come):

Recall is one of the most important commands for behavior control, as it allows you to call your dog back to you in any situation. A dog with a reliable recall is much easier to manage in high-stress situations, as it can be removed from the source of the problem quickly.

- **Training Tip**: Practice recall in a variety of environments, starting with low-distraction areas and gradually working up to more challenging settings, such as parks or busy streets.

- **Practical Example**: If your dog starts chasing after a jogger or cyclist, a strong recall command will bring the dog back to you before the situation escalates.

### 4. "Place":

The "place" command teaches your dog to go to a designated spot, such as a bed or mat, and stay there until released. This command is especially useful for controlling movement and reducing reactivity in the home.

- Training Tip: Begin by teaching your dog to go to its "place" on command, and gradually increase the length of time it stays there. Use treats or toys to encourage calm behavior while the dog is on its mat or bed.

- Practical Example: When guests enter your home, instructing your dog to go to its "place" can prevent it from rushing the door and displaying territorial aggression.

## Building Focus and Impulse Control

Focus and impulse control are critical skills for managing aggressive or reactive dogs. Dogs that struggle with reactivity often lack the ability to control their impulses, especially when faced with a trigger. By teaching your dog to focus on you and practice self-control, you can significantly reduce the likelihood of reactive outbursts.

## Techniques to Build Impulse Control and Focus on the Owner

### 1. Look at Me / Focus Command:

Teaching your dog to focus on you in distracting environments is a key part of managing reactivity. The "look at me" command encourages the dog to make eye contact, shifting its focus away from potential triggers and onto you.

- **Training Tip**: Start in a quiet environment with no distractions. Hold a treat near your eyes and say, "look at me." When your dog makes eye contact, reward it immediately. Gradually increase the difficulty by practicing in more distracting environments, such as when other dogs are nearby.

- **Practical Example**: If your dog becomes fixated on a passing dog or person, the "look at me" command helps redirect its attention, preventing a reactive response.

## 2. Impulse Control Exercises:

Impulse control exercises teach your dog to wait and think before reacting. These exercises help curb the instinct to act immediately, especially in stressful or exciting situations.

- **Wait for Food**: One of the simplest ways to teach impulse control is by asking your dog to wait before eating. Place the food bowl on the ground and ask your dog to "wait." Only release it to eat once it's calm. This teaches patience and self-control.

- **Doorway Exercises**: Many dogs rush through doors, whether to greet someone or explore outside. Teach your dog to "wait" at doorways until given permission to move. This reduces over excitement and helps manage impulsive behaviors like charging at guests or bolting outdoors.

## 3. Structured Play Sessions:

Playtime is a great opportunity to teach impulse control. Games like fetch, tug-of-war, or hide-and-seek can be used to reinforce commands like "sit," "stay," or "drop it." Pausing the game and asking for a command mid-play helps the dog learn to control its excitement and listen even in stimulating situations.

- **Training Tip**: During playtime, periodically ask your dog to stop and sit before continuing. This helps the dog practice impulse control while still having fun.

- **Practical Example**: If your dog is too excited during play and starts to get overstimulated, asking for a quick "sit" or "stay" can reset the dog's focus and prevent any rough behavior from escalating.

## Games and Exercises

1. **Settle on Command**:

Teaching your dog to "settle" or "relax" on command can be a valuable tool for managing high-energy or reactive dogs. This command encourages the dog to lie down and remain calm in stressful situations.

- **Training Tip**: Use this command during moments of calm, such as after a walk or during quiet time at home. Gradually increase the difficulty by using it in more stimulating environments, like a park or during a playdate with other dogs.

- **Practical Example**: If your dog becomes overstimulated during a walk, asking it to "settle" helps lower its energy levels and regain focus.

2. **Impulse Control Games (Like "It's Your Choice")**:

This game teaches your dog to control its impulses by rewarding patience and self-restraint. To play "It's Your Choice," hold treats in your hand and present them to your dog. If the dog tries to grab the treats, close your hand and wait. Only reward the dog when it waits calmly and resists the temptation to snatch the treats.

- **Training Tip**: Gradually increase the difficulty by holding treats in front of the dog's face and rewarding only when it shows restraint. This exercise helps reinforce impulse control in a simple, repeatable way.

- **Practical Example**: Use this game before meals or treats to teach your dog to remain calm and patient in everyday situations.

3. **Tug-of-War with Rules**:

Tug-of-war can be a great way to burn off energy, but it also presents an opportunity to teach impulse control and reinforce important commands. By incorporating rules into tug-of-war, such as pausing the game with a "drop it" or "leave it" command, you can turn playtime into a training exercise that improves your dog's ability to remain calm and controlled.

- **Training Tip**: Start the game of tug with a verbal cue like "take it," and during the game, periodically ask your dog to "drop it." Reward your dog when it releases the toy on command, then start the game again. This helps the dog learn that stopping the game doesn't mean it's over forever—it's just a break.

- **Practical Example**: If your dog gets too excited during a tug game and starts to play too rough, having a solid "drop it" command can help prevent the excitement from turning into over-arousal or aggressive behavior.

## Tools for Success

Training a dog, especially one that is reactive or prone to aggression, often requires the use of specific tools to ensure safety and success. The right equipment can help manage a dog's behavior during training sessions and everyday interactions, giving both the dog and the owner more confidence in stressful situations.

## Recommended Training Tools:

1. **Leashes**:A sturdy leash is one of the most basic, yet essential tools for dog training. For reactive dogs, a leash offers control and safety, ensuring the dog can't suddenly lunge or run toward a trigger.

- **Standard Leash**: A 4- to 6-foot leash is ideal for training, giving you enough control without allowing the dog to stray too far. It's long enough for freedom but short enough to manage reactivity.

- **Training Tip**: When working with a reactive dog, keep the leash short and maintain close control during high-stress situations, such as walks in busy areas or when passing other dogs.

- **Practical Example**: If your dog is reactive toward other dogs during walks, using a short leash can help you prevent lunging and give your dog clear guidance.

**2. Harnesses**:

Harnesses are a safe and effective alternative to collars, especially for dogs prone to pulling or lunging. A harness distributes pressure across the dog's body, reducing the risk of injury and giving the owner more control.

- **Front-Clip Harness**: A front-clip harness helps reduce pulling by turning the dog toward you when it tries to pull forward. This is particularly useful for reactive dogs that lunge toward other dogs, people, or stimuli.

- **Training Tip**: Use a front-clip harness during walks to maintain control over your dog's movements without putting strain on its neck. The harness can also prevent the dog from gaining momentum when lunging.

- **Practical Example**: For a dog that reacts aggressively when it sees other dogs on a walk, a front-clip harness makes it easier to redirect its attention back to you, preventing escalation.

**3. Crates**:

Crates serve as a valuable training tool, providing a safe space for dogs to retreat to when they feel overwhelmed. They can also be used to manage a dog's environment, especially when guests visit or when the dog needs to rest and calm down.

- **Training Tip**: Introduce the crate as a positive, comforting space. Place treats or toys inside to encourage your dog to enter willingly. Never use the crate as a form of punishment, as this will create negative associations.

- **Practical Example**: If your dog becomes reactive when guests enter your home, placing it in a crate with a favorite toy or chew can help reduce anxiety and prevent aggressive behavior. Over time, the crate can become a safe zone for your dog to relax when it feels overstimulated.

**4. Muzzles**:

Muzzles are sometimes necessary for dogs that have a history of biting or are likely to react aggressively in certain situations. While some owners feel hesitant about using muzzles, they can be a helpful tool when introduced correctly and used appropriately.

- **Training Tip**: Introduce the muzzle gradually, allowing your dog to sniff and investigate it before putting it on. Start by placing treats inside the muzzle to create positive associations. Only leave the muzzle on for short periods initially, gradually increasing the time as the dog becomes more comfortable.

- **Practical Example**: If your dog is reactive during veterinary visits or when strangers approach, a muzzle can provide an added layer of safety while ensuring that the dog, the owner, and others around remain calm and secure.

## The Appropriate Use of Safety Tools During Training

### 1. Using Tools to Prevent Escalation:

Safety tools like leashes, harnesses, and muzzles are not meant to restrict your dog's freedom but rather to prevent dangerous situations from escalating. When used appropriately, these tools help your dog learn in a controlled, safe environment, reducing the risk of aggressive outbursts or injury.

- **Leash Use**: In high-stress situations, such as crowded areas or during exposure to a known trigger, keeping your dog on a short leash ensures that you can intervene before the dog reacts aggressively.

- **Muzzle Use**: A muzzle can provide peace of mind when working with a dog that has a history of biting. When your dog is in a new or unpredictable situation, such as a vet visit or socialization session, the muzzle serves as a safeguard, allowing the dog to experience the situation without the risk of injury to others.

## 2. Building Positive Associations:

Whether it's a harness, leash, crate, or muzzle, the key to using any training tool effectively is creating positive associations. Dogs should view these tools as part of a positive, rewarding experience rather than as restrictive or punitive measures.

- **Training Tip**: Use treats, praise, and toys to reward your dog for calmly wearing a harness or muzzle or for resting in its crate. The goal is to ensure the dog feels comfortable and secure, even when wearing or using these tools.

## 3. Gradual Introduction and Desensitization:

Introduce new tools slowly and with patience. If your dog is not used to wearing a muzzle or harness, desensitize it by practicing short, positive sessions where the dog associates the tool with treats and affection.

- **Practical Example**: If your dog has never worn a muzzle before, start by placing the muzzle near its face and rewarding calm behavior. Gradually progress to placing the muzzle on for a few seconds, rewarding the dog at each step, until it can comfortably wear the muzzle for longer periods.

Building a strong training foundation is essential for any dog, but it's particularly crucial for dogs that struggle with aggression or reactivity.

By focusing on basic obedience, teaching commands like "sit," "stay," "recall," and "place," and reinforcing impulse control through structured play and games, you can give your dog the skills it needs to navigate the world more calmly and confidently.

The tools you use—whether it's a leash, harness, crate, or muzzle—are essential for maintaining control and safety during training. When used correctly and paired with positive reinforcement, these tools help prevent aggression and provide your dog with clear guidance in stressful situations.

Ultimately, a well-trained dog is a happier dog. With a solid foundation in obedience and impulse control, your dog will feel more secure in its environment, reducing anxiety and minimizing the likelihood of aggressive or reactive behavior.

As the bond between you and your dog strengthens, both of you will enjoy a more peaceful, fulfilling relationship built on trust, communication, and mutual respect.

# Chapter 6

# Desensitization and Counter-Conditioning

When it comes to managing a dog's aggressive or reactive behavior, two of the most effective techniques are desensitization and counter-conditioning. These methods aim to change the way a dog responds to certain triggers, helping it develop new, calmer reactions.

Rather than suppressing unwanted behavior through punishment, desensitization and counter-conditioning work by addressing the root cause of the behavior—fear, anxiety, or frustration—and gradually shifting the dog's emotional response to something more positive.

This chapter explores what desensitization and counter-conditioning are, how they work, and how to apply them in practical scenarios. These techniques, when used consistently and with patience, can help dogs overcome fear-based reactions and lead more confident, peaceful lives.

## What is Desensitization?

Desensitization is a training technique that involves gradually exposing a dog to the stimuli that trigger its fear or aggression. The key to desensitization is that the exposure must be controlled and incremental, so the dog can remain calm throughout the process. Over time, the dog becomes less sensitive to the trigger, and the once-fearful or aggressive response fades away.

## Gradual Exposure to Triggers to Reduce Fear and Aggression

Desensitization works by allowing the dog to experience the trigger at a level that doesn't cause a significant reaction. The process begins at a distance or intensity where the dog notices the trigger but does not become overwhelmed. As the dog remains calm, the exposure is gradually increased, either by moving closer to the trigger or making the situation slightly more challenging.

1. **Understanding the Process**:

To successfully desensitize a dog, you must start with very mild versions of the trigger. For example:

- If the dog is reactive to other dogs, you would start by exposing it to a calm dog at a considerable distance.

- If the dog is fearful of loud noises, you might begin with very faint sounds, such as the sound of a vacuum in another room.

2. **The Importance of Staying Below the Threshold:**
The critical concept in desensitization is working below the dog's "threshold"—the point at which the dog becomes too anxious or reactive to focus on learning. If the dog is exposed to the trigger at too high a level too soon, it will likely regress or become even more reactive. Staying below the threshold allows the dog to learn and feel more confident with each step.

3. **Slow and Steady Wins the Race**:
Desensitization is a gradual process, often requiring weeks or even months of consistent training to achieve significant results. Trying to rush the process by increasing the intensity of the exposure too quickly can lead to setbacks. However, when done properly, desensitization leads to lasting changes in behavior because the dog learns that the trigger is not something to fear or react aggressively to.

## Steps to Implement Desensitization

### 1. Identify the Trigger:

The first step in desensitizing a dog is to clearly identify what triggers its fear or aggression. This could be a specific object (like a vacuum cleaner), a sound (like fireworks), a person (like the mail carrier), or another dog. It's essential to pinpoint the exact source of the reaction because this will guide the rest of the training process.

### 2. Determine the Dog's Threshold:

Before starting desensitization, you need to find the point where the dog can observe the trigger without reacting. This is the "threshold" level. For example, if your dog reacts to other dogs, find a distance where your dog can see another dog without showing signs of stress (such as barking, lunging, or stiffening). This might be 100 feet away at first.

### 3. Start with Controlled Exposure:

Begin exposing your dog to the trigger at the threshold level, where it is aware of the trigger but remains calm. This could involve walking your dog at a distance where it can see the trigger or playing a recording of a noise at a very low volume. Keep the dog in this calm state while it is exposed to the trigger.

### 4. Gradually Increase Exposure:

As your dog becomes comfortable at the initial threshold, you can gradually reduce the distance or increase the intensity of the trigger. This might mean walking slightly closer to another dog, increasing the volume of a sound, or bringing the vacuum cleaner a little nearer. Continue rewarding calm behavior as you progress.

### 5. Monitor Progress and Adjust:

If your dog begins to show signs of stress or reactivity, you've likely increased the exposure too quickly. Go back to the previous threshold where the dog was calm and successful, and continue the process from there.

# What is Counter-Conditioning?

While desensitization works by reducing the dog's sensitivity to a trigger, counter-conditioning focuses on changing the dog's emotional response to the trigger. Through counter-conditioning, a dog learns to associate the previously feared or disliked stimulus with something positive, such as food, play, or affection. Over time, the negative emotional reaction is replaced with a more positive one.

## Pairing Triggers with Positive Experiences to Change the Dog's Emotional Response

Counter-conditioning works by essentially rewiring the dog's brain to see the trigger in a new, positive light. For example:

- A dog that is fearful of other dogs can learn to associate the sight of another dog with receiving treats.

- A dog that reacts aggressively to strangers can be conditioned to expect praise or playtime when strangers are near.

The process involves presenting the trigger in a controlled way and immediately pairing it with a reward. Over time, the dog begins to anticipate something good whenever it encounters the trigger, which helps reduce the initial fear or aggression.

1. **Creating Positive Associations**:

To successfully counter-condition your dog, you need to ensure that the trigger is consistently paired with a reward the dog loves. This could be high-value treats, a favorite toy, or enthusiastic praise. The reward must be something the dog finds exciting or pleasurable.

- **Timing is Everything**: The timing of the reward is crucial in counter-conditioning. The reward should be given as soon as the dog sees or hears the trigger, before the dog has a chance to react negatively.

This helps the dog link the presence of the trigger with something positive.

### 2. Consistency and Repetition:

Just like desensitization, counter-conditioning requires consistency and repetition. Every time the dog encounters the trigger, it should be paired with something positive. Over time, the dog's brain rewires its response, expecting a reward instead of feeling fear or aggression.

## Steps to Implement Counter-Conditioning

### 1. Set Up for Success:

Start with a mild version of the trigger, similar to desensitization. The goal is to present the trigger in a way that doesn't overwhelm the dog but still allows it to notice the stimulus. For example, if your dog is reactive to loud noises, play a sound at a very low volume and immediately offer a treat.

### 2. Pair the Trigger with a Reward:

Each time the dog sees or hears the trigger, immediately give a reward. The reward needs to be delivered right as the dog becomes aware of the trigger but before it has time to react negatively. This process may need to be repeated dozens of times before the dog starts to anticipate the reward in the presence of the trigger.

### 3. Gradually Increase the Intensity of the Trigger:

As your dog begins to associate the trigger with positive outcomes, you can slowly increase the intensity of the trigger. This might mean decreasing the distance between your dog and another dog, raising the volume of a noise, or bringing a feared object closer. Continue pairing the trigger with rewards at each stage.

### 4. Use High-Value Rewards:

It's essential to use high-value rewards during counter-conditioning sessions. Regular kibble might not be enough to distract a fearful or reactive dog, especially in the early stages. Consider using special treats like small pieces of chicken, cheese, or a favorite toy. The more your dog loves the reward, the stronger the association will be.

**5. Reinforce Positive Behavior in Everyday Situations**:

Beyond structured counter-conditioning sessions, you can reinforce the new, positive associations in everyday situations. For example:

- If your dog encounters a trigger during a walk and remains calm, reward it immediately with a treat or praise.

- If the dog stays composed when a visitor comes to the door, provide a reward to reinforce the positive behavior.

## Combining Desensitization and Counter-Conditioning

Desensitization and counter-conditioning are often used together to achieve the best results. Desensitization helps the dog remain calm in the presence of a trigger, while counter-conditioning shifts the dog's emotional response to something positive. By using both techniques, you can gradually reduce your dog's sensitivity to triggers and replace fear or aggression with calmness and anticipation of rewards.

For example, if your dog is reactive to other dogs:

- **Desensitization**: Begin by walking your dog at a distance where it can see another dog but remain calm. Over time, decrease the distance.

- **Counter-Conditioning**: Each time your dog sees another dog, offer it a treat before it has a chance to react negatively. Over time, your dog will learn to expect something good when it sees another dog, which reduces its reactive behavior.

## Practical Example:

Let's take the example of a dog named Rex, who becomes aggressive whenever someone knocks on the door.

1. **Desensitization**:

The first step is to desensitize Rex to the sound of knocking. His owner starts by having a friend knock very softly on the door from outside. Rex is kept calm at a distance from the door, and each time he hears the knock, the owner rewards him for remaining quiet and composed. Over time, the knocks become louder, and Rex learns to stay calm at each new level of exposure.

**2. Counter-Conditioning**:

At the same time, Rex's owner begins pairing the knock with something positive. Each time Rex hears the knock, he receives a treat. Eventually, Rex starts to associate the sound of knocking with getting a reward. Instead of reacting aggressively, he begins to look to his owner for a treat whenever someone knocks on the door.

After several weeks of consistent training using desensitization and counter-conditioning, Rex's aggressive behavior at the sound of knocking diminishes. He no longer perceives the knock as a threat and instead associates it with positive experiences.

Desensitization and counter-conditioning are powerful tools in managing and modifying aggressive or reactive behavior in dogs. These methods work by gradually exposing the dog to triggers in a controlled way and pairing those triggers with positive rewards. Unlike punishment-based approaches, these techniques address the underlying emotions driving the behavior—fear, anxiety, or frustration—helping the dog feel more comfortable and secure in stressful situations.

While these techniques require time, consistency, and patience, they offer a long-term solution to behavioral issues by changing the way your dog feels about its triggers. By using desensitization and counter-conditioning, you can help your dog lead a more relaxed, confident life and improve your bond in the process.

Desensitization and counter-conditioning are incredibly effective techniques for modifying a dog's behavior, but they require a systematic approach to ensure success. Understanding the steps involved and gauging your dog's progress will help prevent frustration for both you and your dog. In this section, we'll walk through a step-by-step guide to implementing these techniques and offer a detailed case study to illustrate how desensitization and counter-conditioning can be applied to a real-life scenario.

## Steps to Implementing Both

Successful desensitization and counter-conditioning depend on following a structured, patient process. The key is to expose your dog to triggers in a way that doesn't overwhelm it, while simultaneously rewarding calm and positive behavior. Let's break down the steps.

## Step 1: Identify Your Dog's Triggers

Before you can begin desensitization or counter-conditioning, you need to identify exactly what triggers your dog's reactive or aggressive behavior. The more specific you can be, the better. Triggers could include:

- **Visual stimuli**: Other dogs, people wearing hats, or children running.

- **Auditory stimuli**: Thunderstorms, doorbells, or loud cars.

- **Tactile stimuli**: Being touched in sensitive areas like the paws or tail.

Once you have identified the triggers, observe how your dog reacts to them. Does your dog become anxious when it sees another dog at a certain distance? Is it triggered by loud noises? This observation will help you figure out how and when to begin the desensitization process.

## Step 2: Determine the Threshold

A dog's threshold is the point at which it reacts to a trigger. If you start desensitizing a dog when it's already highly agitated, it's too late for the learning process to be effective. Therefore, your goal is to determine your dog's threshold and work below it.

For example, if your dog barks and lunges when it sees another dog within 20 feet, its threshold might be around 25 feet. At this distance, the dog notices the other dog but does not yet react aggressively. Working within this "safe zone" is where desensitization begins.

## Step 3: Create a Controlled Environment

You'll want to begin training in a controlled, low-stress environment where you can manage your dog's exposure to its triggers. If your dog is reactive to other dogs, start training in an area where you can control the distance between your dog and other dogs—such as a quiet park or a backyard with distant visual access to the stimulus.

If your dog reacts to noises, play the sound at a low volume inside your home. The idea is to create a situation where your dog can encounter the trigger but still remain calm.

## Step 4: Start with Desensitization

Begin exposing your dog to the trigger at a low intensity, just enough for the dog to notice but not enough to provoke a reaction. For example:

- **Distance**: If your dog is reactive to other dogs, begin at a distance where your dog sees the other dog but does not react. This might be 50 feet away.

- **Volume**: If the trigger is a sound, start with a very low volume and gradually increase the intensity.

During this step, keep your dog calm. If your dog becomes tense or shows signs of stress, you need to move back or decrease the intensity of the trigger. The dog should remain below its threshold at all times during this phase of training.

## Step 5: Introduce Counter-Conditioning

As soon as your dog notices the trigger, start counter-conditioning by rewarding it with something highly desirable. This could be a favorite treat, praise, or playtime. The reward should immediately follow the trigger to create a positive association. For example:

- If your dog sees another dog in the distance but stays calm, offer it a treat right away.

- If your dog hears a loud noise at a low volume and does not react, praise and reward it with treats.

The goal is to teach your dog that the trigger predicts something enjoyable, which will gradually change its emotional response from fear or aggression to excitement or neutrality.

## Step 6: Gradually Increase the Intensity of the Trigger

Over time, as your dog becomes more comfortable with the trigger at its initial intensity, you can gradually increase the difficulty:

- **Reduce the Distance**: Move closer to the trigger while ensuring your dog stays calm. For example, if you started at 50 feet away from another dog, try moving to 40 feet after several successful sessions.

- **Increase the Volume or Frequency**: If your dog reacts to a sound, slowly increase the volume over several sessions. Continue to reward your dog for staying calm.

Remember, the process should be gradual. If your dog starts to react negatively, go back to the previous step where it was successful.

## Step 7: Monitor and Adjust

Throughout the training process, it's important to monitor your dog's reactions and adjust accordingly. Pay close attention to your dog's body language. If you see signs of anxiety (such as panting, pacing, or freezing), you've likely progressed too quickly. Go back to the point where your dog was comfortable and continue at that level until your dog is ready to move forward again.

## Step 8: Consistency is Key

Desensitization and counter-conditioning are not quick fixes. They require consistent effort and patience over time. Training should be done in short, frequent sessions—ideally every day or several times a week. The more consistent you are, the more likely your dog will be to generalize the new, positive associations across different environments and situations.

## Identifying the Correct Pace for Your Dog's Progress

One of the most important aspects of desensitization and counter-conditioning is identifying the correct pace for your dog. Moving too quickly can overwhelm your dog and cause setbacks, while moving too slowly may not show noticeable progress. Here are some tips to ensure you're progressing at the right pace.

1. **Observe Your Dog's Reactions**:

The best way to gauge your dog's readiness to progress is by closely observing its behavior during training sessions. If your dog stays calm, is able to focus on you, and eagerly takes rewards, it's likely ready to take the next step. On the other hand, if your dog shows signs of stress (such as lip licking, yawning, or stiff body posture), it's a sign that you need to slow down or go back to the previous step.

2. **Don't Rush**:

The most common mistake in desensitization and counter-conditioning is trying to move too quickly. If your dog is doing well at one distance, don't immediately cut the distance in half. Instead, make small incremental changes, such as moving forward by just a few feet each session.

**3. Look for Generalization**:

Before increasing the intensity of the trigger, ensure that your dog's new positive response is consistent across multiple situations. For example, if your dog is calm around other dogs at 30 feet in a quiet park, try practicing in a different setting, such as a busier street, before moving closer to the trigger.

**4. Celebrate Small Wins**:

Progress may seem slow, but even small improvements are important. If your dog can walk calmly past another dog at a distance of 40 feet when it used to react at 50 feet, that's progress worth celebrating. Acknowledging these small victories will help keep you motivated and focused on the long-term goal.

**5. Use Breaks Effectively**:

Training can be stressful for both you and your dog, so it's essential to include breaks during the process. Short, focused sessions of 10 to 15 minutes are usually more effective than longer sessions. Give your dog plenty of time to relax and unwind between training exercises.

## Case Study:

Let's look at a detailed example of how these techniques can be applied to a real-life scenario with a reactive dog named Charlie.

## Background:

Charlie is a four-year-old Border Collie mix who becomes reactive whenever he sees other dogs during walks. His owner, Jane, has struggled with his behavior for years. When Charlie sees another dog, he barks, lunges, and pulls on the leash, making walks stressful and unpredictable. Jane wants to help Charlie learn to stay calm around other dogs.

## Step 1: Identify the Trigger

Through careful observation, Jane determines that Charlie's reactivity is triggered by the sight of other dogs. His threshold—the point at which he begins to bark and lunge—is around 50 feet. At any distance closer than that, Charlie becomes difficult to manage.

## Step 2: Create a Controlled Environment

Jane decides to start Charlie's training in a nearby park that is large enough for her to keep a safe distance from other dogs. She schedules their walks during quieter times of the day when fewer dogs are present. This controlled environment allows Jane to introduce Charlie to other dogs at a distance while maintaining his focus.

## Step 3: Begin Desensitization

Jane begins walking Charlie at a distance of 60 feet from other dogs, which is beyond his threshold. At this distance, Charlie can see the other dogs but does not react. Jane keeps Charlie calm by speaking to him in a soothing voice and rewarding him with treats for walking calmly.

## Step 4: Introduce Counter-Conditioning

Whenever Charlie spots another dog in the distance and stays calm, Jane immediately gives him a high-value treat (small pieces of chicken, which Charlie loves). The sight of another dog becomes a signal for something positive, rather than a reason to react aggressively.

## Step 5: Gradually Increase Exposure

Over the next few weeks, Jane gradually decreases the distance between Charlie and other dogs. First, she moves to 50 feet, then 40 feet, and eventually 30 feet. At each new distance, Jane ensures that Charlie remains calm and focused on her before rewarding him. If Charlie begins to show signs of stress, Jane increases the distance again to keep him below his threshold.

## Step 6: Monitor Progress

Jane notices that after several weeks of consistent training, Charlie no longer barks or lunges at dogs that are 30 feet away. He has learned to associate the sight of other dogs with positive experiences, and his overall anxiety around other dogs has decreased. Jane continues to monitor his progress and occasionally increases the challenge by practicing in busier areas.

## Step 7: Test in Different Environments

Once Charlie has successfully learned to remain calm around dogs in the quiet park, Jane starts practicing in different environments. She walks him in a busier area where more dogs are present but maintains the same gradual approach. Charlie's new behavior generalizes across different situations, and Jane continues to reinforce his calm demeanor with treats and praise.

Desensitization and counter-conditioning require patience, consistency, and a thorough understanding of your dog's triggers and threshold. By following a structured approach, you can help your dog overcome fear, anxiety, and aggression while fostering a more positive emotional response to its triggers. This process may take time, but the long-term benefits of having a calm, confident dog make the effort worthwhile.

In the case study of Charlie, his owner Jane was able to successfully reduce his reactivity by combining desensitization with counter-conditioning and working at a pace that suited Charlie's progress. With time and dedication, any dog owner can achieve similar results, helping their dog lead a happier, less reactive life.

# Chapter 7

# Addressing Specific Types of Aggression

When it comes to managing dog aggression, understanding the root cause of the behavior is essential. Aggression can take many forms, but two of the most common types are fear-based aggression and resource guarding. Each of these behaviors is driven by different emotions and instincts, requiring targeted strategies for improvement. In this chapter, we'll explore the causes and signs of fear-based aggression and resource guarding, along with specific techniques to address and reduce these behaviors.

## Fear-Based Aggression

Fear-based aggression occurs when a dog reacts aggressively in response to something it perceives as a threat. Unlike dominance or territorial aggression, which might stem from a desire to assert control, fear-based aggression is driven by the dog's need to defend itself from what it views as danger. In many cases, the dog feels cornered or anxious and lashes out because it sees no other way to escape the situation.

## Causes and Signs of Fear-Based Aggression

**Causes**:

Fear-based aggression can arise from various situations and experiences, such as:

- **Lack of socialization**: Dogs that were not properly socialized as puppies may develop fear-based aggression because they are unfamiliar with people, other dogs, or new environments.

- **Trauma or abuse**: Dogs that have been mistreated, neglected, or subjected to traumatic experiences may become fearful of certain people, objects, or situations. Their aggression is a defensive response to protect themselves from perceived harm.

- **Negative experiences**: A single bad experience, such as being attacked by another dog or frightened by a loud noise, can trigger fear-based aggression. This often leads to heightened sensitivity around similar triggers in the future.

- **Genetics and temperament**: Some dogs are naturally more anxious or fearful due to their genetic makeup. Breeds that are more nervous or sensitive may be more prone to fear-based aggression if not carefully managed.

**Signs**:

Dogs exhibiting fear-based aggression often display certain body language cues and behaviors that indicate their fear:

- **Cowering or backing away**: Fearful dogs may try to make themselves smaller by lowering their bodies, tucking their tails, or backing away from the perceived threat.

- **Raised hackles**: The hair along the dog's back, from neck to tail, may stand on end, a clear sign that the dog feels threatened.

- **Growling or snapping**: Growling is often an early warning signal that the dog is uncomfortable. If pushed too far, the dog may snap as a way to protect itself.

- **Avoidance of eye contact**: Dogs that are scared often avoid direct eye contact, which can be seen as confrontational. They may also avert their gaze or look toward an escape route.

- **Lip licking, yawning, or panting**: These are common signs of stress and anxiety in dogs. A dog that exhibits these behaviors might be trying to self-soothe in an uncomfortable situation.

## Techniques for Fear-Driven Behavior

When dealing with fear-based aggression, the primary goal is to help the dog feel safe and secure in situations that would normally trigger its fear response. This can be accomplished through a combination of behavior modification techniques, careful management, and building trust.

### 1. Desensitization and Counter-Conditioning:

As discussed in earlier chapters, desensitization and counter-conditioning are powerful tools for reducing fear-based aggression. By gradually exposing the dog to its triggers at a low intensity and pairing these exposures with positive reinforcement (like treats or praise), the dog learns to associate the trigger with positive experiences rather than fear.

- **Practical Example**: If a dog is fearful of strangers, start by having the dog observe a stranger from a distance at which the dog remains calm. Reward the dog with treats for staying relaxed. Over time, decrease the distance, always ensuring the dog remains below its threshold of fear.

### 2. Create a Safe-Space:

Dogs with fear-based aggression often benefit from having a designated "safe space" where they can retreat when they feel anxious. This could be a crate, a specific room, or a quiet corner in the house. The safe space should be off-limits to other pets or people when the dog is using it.

- **Practical Example**: If a dog becomes overwhelmed during family gatherings, set up its crate in a quiet room with comforting items like its favorite toys or a blanket. Teach the dog that this space is where it can go to feel secure whenever it's anxious.

### 3. Avoid Forcing Interactions:

Never force a fearful dog into situations that make it uncomfortable. Forcing a dog to confront its fears head-on, such as making it interact with strangers or other dogs before it's ready, can worsen its anxiety and increase aggressive responses.

- **Practical Example**: If a dog is scared of other dogs, avoid dog parks or places with off-leash dogs until the dog has made progress with desensitization. Instead, focus on calm, controlled exposure at a distance that doesn't trigger fear.

### 4. Build Confidence Through Training:

Training and obedience work can help build a dog's confidence, which can reduce fear-based aggression over time. Training creates structure and predictability in the dog's life, making it feel more secure.

- **Practical Example**: Teach the dog basic obedience commands like "sit," "stay," and "leave it." These commands give the dog something to focus on in stressful situations and help the dog learn that it can rely on you for guidance.

### 5. Gradual Socialization:

For dogs that were not well-socialized as puppies, slow and careful socialization with new people, dogs, and environments can help reduce fear. However, this must be done gradually and with positive reinforcement.

- **Practical Example**: Introduce the dog to new people in a calm, quiet setting. Start with one person at a time, allowing the dog to approach at its own pace. Reward the dog for calm behavior and gradually increase the complexity of the interactions.

## Resource Guarding

Resource guarding occurs when a dog becomes protective or defensive over items it values, such as food, toys, or even its favorite resting spot. While this behavior is natural in many animals, it can become problematic in domestic dogs, especially if it leads to aggressive actions like growling, snapping, or biting.

## Why Dogs Guard Food, Toys, and Spaces

### Evolutionary Instincts:

Resource guarding is rooted in survival instincts. In the wild, animals must protect their food and other valuable resources from competitors. While domestic dogs no longer need to compete for survival, the instinct to guard what they value is still present.

### Lack of Early Socialization:

Puppies that are not exposed to shared feeding or that are raised in environments where they had to compete for resources may develop guarding behaviors as adults. Early socialization around food, toys, and space-sharing can help reduce the likelihood of resource guarding later on.

### Fear of Losing Valuable Items:

Some dogs guard resources because they are afraid of losing them. If a dog has had food or toys taken away in the past, it may react aggressively to protect these items. Insecure dogs may feel that they must defend their resources to ensure they won't lose them.

## Guarding People or Space:

In some cases, dogs may guard their favorite person or resting spot. This is often a sign that the dog views these resources as particularly important and doesn't want others to have access.

## Training Exercises to Eliminate Resource Guarding

### 1. Trading Up:

One of the most effective ways to eliminate resource guarding is to teach the dog that giving up a valued resource results in receiving something even better. This technique, known as "trading up," helps the dog learn that relinquishing control doesn't mean losing out—it means gaining something even more rewarding.

- **Practical Example**: If a dog guards its food bowl, approach the dog while it's eating and drop a high-value treat (like a piece of chicken) into the bowl. This teaches the dog that your presence near the food bowl brings good things, rather than posing a threat.

### 2. Leave It and Drop It Commands:

Teaching the dog "leave it" and "drop it" commands can help prevent resource guarding before it escalates. These commands give the dog a clear signal to relinquish an object and trust that something good will happen afterward.

- **Practical Example**: Use a favorite toy to practice the "drop it" command. When the dog releases the toy on command, reward it with a treat or praise. Over time, the dog will learn to let go of items without feeling the need to guard them.

### 3. Desensitization Around Resources:

Just as desensitization can help with fear-based aggression, it can also be effective in reducing resource guarding. By gradually getting the dog used to your presence near its valued resources without taking them away, you can decrease the dog's defensive behavior.

- **Practical Example**: If a dog guards its toys, start by sitting a few feet away while the dog plays with the toy. Gradually move closer, always rewarding the dog for remaining calm. Over time, the dog will become more comfortable with your presence around its toys.

**4. Hand-Feeding:**

For dogs that guard their food bowls, hand-feeding can help reduce the impulse to guard. By feeding the dog directly from your hand, you create a positive association between your presence and receiving food.

- **Practical Example**: Start by feeding small portions of the dog's meal from your hand, one piece at a time. This teaches the dog that you are the source of the food and that there's no need to guard the bowl.

**5. Establishing Clear Boundaries:**

Establishing boundaries around resources helps the dog understand that it doesn't need to guard specific items from its human family members. This can be done by teaching the dog that you control the resources and that it will receive them at appropriate times.

- **Practical Example**: Before giving the dog access to food, toys, or treats, ask it to perform a command like "sit" or "stay." This reinforces the idea that you are in control of the resources, and the dog will learn to associate calm behavior with receiving the items it values.

**6. Remove Triggers if Necessary:**

In some cases, it might be helpful to remove triggers temporarily while working on resource-guarding behavior. For example, suppose two dogs in a household compete over toys. In that case, it may be helpful to separate them during playtime until both dogs have improved in their guarding behaviors.

- **Practical Example**: If a dog guards its bed from other pets or people, move the bed to a different location and work on desensitizing the dog to others approaching its resting spot, gradually rewarding it for calm behavior when others come near.

## Reducing Anxiety Around Resources

In many cases, resource guarding is driven by anxiety or insecurity. It's important to reduce this anxiety so the dog feels less of a need to defend its valued items. Creating an environment where the dog feels secure and knows that resources are plentiful can help eliminate guarding behaviors.

1. **Routine Feeding and Play Schedules**:

Establishing a predictable routine helps dogs feel secure. If the dog knows it will be fed at certain times and that toys will be available during designated play sessions, it's less likely to feel the need to guard resources out of fear of scarcity.

- **Practical Example**: Feed the dog at the same times every day and provide regular play sessions where the dog has access to toys. This consistency reduces anxiety and helps the dog feel secure in its environment.

**2. Avoid Punishment:**

Punishing a dog for resource guarding can backfire by increasing its anxiety and reinforcing the guarding behavior. Instead, focus on positive reinforcement, rewarding the dog for calm behavior around resources.

- **Practical Example**: If the dog starts to guard its toys or food, don't punish or yell. Instead, calmly remove the resource if necessary, and then work on desensitization or the "drop it" command to reduce the guarding behavior.

Fear-based aggression and resource guarding are two common forms of aggression in dogs, but they are manageable with the right approach. By understanding the causes of these behaviors and using targeted techniques like desensitization, counter-conditioning, and positive reinforcement, you can help your dog feel more secure and reduce its aggressive tendencies.

Fear-based aggression often stems from a lack of confidence, past trauma, or negative experiences. Helping your dog overcome this requires patience, trust-building, and gradual exposure to feared triggers. Meanwhile, resource guarding is a natural behavior that can be addressed through training exercises that teach the dog to relinquish control and trust its owner around valued items.

With consistent training, a calm environment, and an understanding of your dog's emotional needs, it's possible to manage and reduce both fear-based aggression and resource guarding, leading to a more peaceful and enjoyable relationship with your dog.

In this section of Chapter 6, we'll focus on two particularly challenging types of aggression: leash aggression (also known as leash reactivity) and dog-to-dog aggression.

Both types of aggression can make daily walks and social interactions stressful, and they often leave dog owners feeling frustrated or embarrassed. However, with the right understanding and training strategies, leash aggression and dog-to-dog aggression can be managed and significantly reduced. This chapter will explore the causes of these behaviors and provide step-by-step training protocols to help your dog remain calm and controlled in challenging situations.

## Leash Aggression

Leash aggression, or leash reactivity, occurs when a dog becomes overly aroused, frustrated, or fearful while on a leash, often leading to barking, lunging, growling, or pulling toward other dogs, people, or objects. This behavior can make walks unpleasant for both the dog and the owner, and it may escalate to more serious aggressive behaviors if not addressed.

## Understanding Leash Reactivity

Leash reactivity often stems from frustration or fear. When a dog is on a leash, it may feel restrained and unable to interact with its environment in the way it wants to. For dogs that are naturally curious or social, the leash can prevent them from engaging with other dogs or people, leading to frustration. For more fearful dogs, the leash can intensify their anxiety because they feel trapped and unable to escape from perceived threats.

## Causes of Leash Reactivity:

1. **Frustration**: Dogs that are highly social or energetic may become frustrated when they are restricted from interacting with other dogs or stimuli. The leash prevents them from moving freely, which leads to reactive behaviors like barking, lunging, or pulling.

2. **Fear or Anxiety**: Some dogs are naturally fearful or have had negative experiences with other dogs or people in the past. The leash restricts their ability to flee from a perceived threat, so they may react aggressively out of fear.

3. **Lack of Socialization**: Dogs that were not properly socialized as puppies may not know how to interact appropriately with other dogs. When restrained on a leash, this lack of experience can lead to confusion, anxiety, or aggressive reactions.

4. **Leash Tension**: A tense leash can signal to the dog that there is something to be concerned about. When owners tighten the leash upon seeing another dog or person, the dog picks up on the tension and may assume the approaching individual or animal is a threat, escalating its reactive behavior.

## Step-by-Step Training Protocols

Addressing leash aggression requires patience and consistent training. The goal is to teach the dog how to remain calm and focused on the owner, even in the presence of triggers like other dogs or people.

### 1. Teaching Focus and Attention on Walks:

One of the first steps in reducing leash reactivity is teaching your dog to focus on you during walks, rather than fixating on other dogs or distractions. This can be done through the "look at me" command, where the dog learns to make eye contact with you when prompted.

- **Training Tip**: Start in a quiet, low-distraction environment. Hold a treat near your eyes and say "look at me." Reward your dog when it makes eye contact. Gradually increase distractions, like walking in busier areas, but continue rewarding the dog for focusing on you.

### 2. Desensitization to Triggers:

Desensitization involves gradually exposing your dog to its triggers (e.g., other dogs) at a distance where it can stay calm. Over time, you can reduce the distance and increase the exposure.

- **Step-by-Step Protocol**:

    - Start in an open space, like a park, where other dogs are present but at a safe distance (outside your dog's reactivity threshold).

    - As soon as your dog notices another dog but remains calm, reward it with a treat.

    - Gradually reduce the distance, rewarding calm behavior at each new level.

    - If your dog starts to react (barking, lunging, etc.), you've moved too close, and you'll need to increase the distance again.

### 3. Counter-Conditioning:

Pairing the presence of other dogs or triggers with positive reinforcement, such as treats or praise, helps your dog form new, positive associations with the stimulus. This reduces the likelihood of aggressive reactions.

- **Training Tip**: Every time your dog sees another dog on a walk and remains calm, offer a high-value reward. Over time, your dog will learn to associate the sight of other dogs with something enjoyable.

### 4. Loose Leash Walking:

Teaching your dog to walk on a loose leash is essential for reducing leash aggression. A tense leash can increase a dog's frustration or anxiety, making reactive behaviors more likely. Loose leash walking allows your dog to remain calm and relaxed.

- **Training Tip**: Practice loose leash walking in low-distraction environments before progressing to areas with more stimuli. Use a front-clip harness to discourage pulling and always reward your dog for walking calmly beside you.

### 5. Teaching "Leave It" and "Heal":

Commands like "leave it" and "heel" are helpful tools for managing leash aggression. "Leave it" teaches the dog to ignore distractions, while "heel" encourages your dog to stay close to you during walks.

- **Training Tip**: Start by practicing these commands in controlled environments before using them during walks. Consistently reward your dog for following commands and staying calm when other dogs or people pass by.

## Dog-to-Dog Aggression

Dog-to-dog aggression can be stressful and dangerous, especially in multi-dog households or during interactions at dog parks. This type of aggression may occur for a variety of reasons, including fear, resource guarding, territoriality, or poor socialization. Understanding the causes and learning how to manage these interactions safely is crucial for creating peaceful relationships between dogs.

## What Causes Dog-to-Dog Aggression?

Dog-to-dog aggression can arise for several reasons, and identifying the cause is essential for developing an effective training plan.

1. **Fear or Anxiety**:

Some dogs react aggressively toward other dogs out of fear. This can happen if the dog has had negative experiences with other dogs in the past or if it feels intimidated by certain types of dogs (e.g., larger or more energetic dogs).

**2. Lack of Socialization**:

Dogs that were not exposed to other dogs as puppies may not know how to interact appropriately. They may misread other dogs' signals or become overwhelmed during interactions, leading to aggressive behaviors.

**3. Resource Guarding**:

Some dogs become aggressive when they feel that their resources (food, toys, or even their owner's attention) are being threatened by another dog. This is particularly common in multi-dog households where dogs may compete for the same resources.

**4. Territorial Behavior**:

Some dogs exhibit territorial aggression, especially when they perceive another dog as invading their space. This can happen in shared environments, like dog parks or even within the home.

**5. Over excitement**:

In some cases, dogs may become overly excited during play with other dogs, and this excitement can escalate into aggressive behavior. This is common in high-energy dogs or those that haven't learned how to moderate their excitement during interactions.

## Safe Management and Training

Whether managing aggression between dogs in a multi-dog household or en-suring safe interactions at a dog park, the key is to be proactive and implement training strategies that promote calm and appropriate behavior.

1. **Structured Introductions**:

When introducing dogs to each other—whether in the home or at a park—it's important to do so in a structured, controlled manner. Avoid allowing dogs to rush at each other or immediately engage in face-to-face greetings, which can be overwhelming or misinterpreted as aggressive.

- **Step-by-Step Protocol for Introductions**:

    - Start by allowing the dogs to observe each other from a distance. This reduces the pressure on both dogs and allows them to get used to each other's presence.

    - Use parallel walking, where the dogs walk side-by-side at a distance without directly interacting. This helps them acclimate to each other in a non-confrontational way.

    - Gradually decrease the distance between the dogs, always monitor-ing for signs of stress or aggression. If either dog shows signs of discomfort, increase the distance and try again later.

2. **Managing Resources in Multi-Dog Households:**

To prevent resource guarding between dogs, it's important to establish clear boundaries and manage resources carefully. Feeding dogs separately and pro-viding individual playtime can help reduce competition and prevent aggressive behaviors.

- **Training Tip**: Feed each dog in a separate room or crate to avoid conflicts over food. During playtime, use different toys for each dog and teach the "drop it" command to ensure the dogs learn to share or relinquish toys without conflict.

### 3. Use Positive Reinforcement for Calm Behavior:

Whether at home or in a public space, rewarding calm, non-aggressive behavior is key to reducing dog-to-dog aggression. Dogs should be rewarded for appropriate greetings, calm play, and relaxed behavior around other dogs.

- **Training Tip**: Bring high-value treats with you to dog parks or when introducing dogs to each other. Reward your dog each time it remains calm or engages in positive interactions with other dogs.

### 4. Supervised Play at Dog Parks:

Dog parks can be a great place for socialization, but they can also be a breeding ground for aggressive behavior if not managed properly. Always supervise your dog closely during play to prevent over excitement or escalating aggression.

- **Training Tip**: If your dog becomes too excited during play, use the "leave it" or "come" command to interrupt the behavior. Give your dog a short break from play to calm down before allowing it to rejoin the group. This helps prevent over excitement from turning into aggression.

### 5. Work on Impulse Control:

Training your dog to control its impulses around other dogs can significantly reduce aggressive behavior.

Commands like "sit," "stay," and "wait" teach your dog to remain calm in the presence of other dogs and to respond to your guidance.

- **Training Tip**: Practice impulse control exercises at home first, then gradually introduce other dogs into the training environment. Start with a calm, familiar dog and increase the challenge as your dog improves.

Leash aggression and dog-to-dog aggression can be challenging behaviors to manage, but with the right training strategies, they can be reduced and even eliminated over time.

Understanding the underlying causes of these behaviors—whether it's fear, frustration, or lack of socialization—helps guide the training process.

# Chapter 8

# Positive Reinforcement Training

P ositive reinforcement training is a powerful and humane approach to behavior modification in dogs, especially when addressing aggression or other
challenging behaviors.

Unlike punishment-based methods, which focus on discouraging unwanted
behavior, positive reinforcement works by rewarding desired behavior, encour-
aging the dog to repeat those actions.

This training method is not only effective but also helps build trust, confidence, and a stronger bond between you and your dog. In this chapter, we'll
explore the principles of reward-based training, why punishment-based methods
often fail in aggressive dogs, and how to create a structured reward system that
works.

## What is Positive Reinforcement?

Positive reinforcement is a training technique where you reward a dog for performing a desired behavior, increasing the likelihood that the behavior will be
repeated. The idea is simple: by associating good behavior with something the

dog values—like treats, toys, or praise—the dog learns to repeat those behaviors to receive the reward.

## The Principles of Reward-Based Training

At its core, positive reinforcement is about focusing on what the dog is doing right rather than punishing it for mistakes. By doing so, the dog is encouraged to make the right choices. Let's break down the key principles that make this approach so effective.

1. **Immediate Rewards**:

For positive reinforcement to work, the reward must be given immediately after the desired behavior occurs. Dogs live in the moment, so if there's a delay between the behavior and the reward, they may not make the connection. For example:

- If you ask your dog to "sit" and it does so, you must reward it right away for sitting. If you wait too long, the dog may not understand what it's being rewarded for.

**2. Consistency is Key:**

Consistency is critical when using positive reinforcement. Every time the dog performs the desired behavior, it should be rewarded. Over time, the dog will learn that behaving a certain way results in good things, making it more likely to repeat the behavior.

- **Practical Example**: If you're working on leash walking and your dog walks beside you without pulling, immediately reward this calm behavior. Doing this consistently will help the dog understand that walking nicely leads to rewards.

**3. Clear Communication:**

Dogs need clear and simple cues to understand what behavior is expected of them. Pairing the behavior with a specific verbal cue (like "sit" or "stay") helps the dog associate the action with the command. Over time, the dog will learn to respond to verbal cues without needing additional prompting.

**4. High-Value Rewards**:

Not all rewards are created equal. To motivate your dog, especially in challenging situations, use high-value rewards that your dog truly loves, such as special treats, toys, or praise. The more the dog enjoys the reward, the more motivated it will be to perform the desired behavior.

- **Practical Example**: If your dog is learning to stay calm around other dogs, use a high-value reward like pieces of chicken to reinforce calm behavior. This reward is more enticing than everyday kibble and will be more effective in getting your dog's attention.

## Why Punishment-Based Methods Often Fail?

While punishment-based methods may seem to provide quick results, they often fail in the long run, especially with aggressive dogs. Punishment can worsen the dog's behavior and damage the relationship between the dog and its owner. Here's why punishment-based training is often ineffective and counterproductive.

1. **Increased Fear and Anxiety**:

Aggression in dogs is often rooted in fear or anxiety. Punishing a dog for aggressive behavior may intensify these feelings, making the dog even more fearful and reactive. Rather than learning to manage its emotions, the dog may become more aggressive in response to the perceived threat of punishment.

- **Practical Example**: If a dog is fearful of strangers and barks aggressively when approached, punishing the dog may increase its fear and anxiety. The dog may associate the punishment with the presence of strangers, worsening the aggressive behavior.

2. **Suppressing Behavior Without Addressing the Cause:**

Punishment may suppress a dog's aggressive behavior temporarily, but it doesn't address the underlying cause of the aggression. The dog may stop growling or barking out of fear of punishment, but the anxiety or frustration driving the behavior remains. Over time, the dog's aggression may escalate because the root cause hasn't been addressed.

- **Practical Example**: A dog that is punished for growling at other dogs may stop growling but could eventually escalate to biting because its underlying fear or frustration hasn't been resolved.

### 3. Damaging the Bond:

Positive reinforcement builds trust between the dog and its owner, while punishment can damage that bond. When a dog is punished, it may begin to associate its owner with negative experiences, leading to fear, mistrust, and further behavioral issues.

- **Practical Example**: If a dog is frequently punished for misbehavior, it may start to avoid its owner or become anxious in the owner's presence, making training more difficult and less effective.

### 4. Escalating Aggression:

In some cases, punishment can cause a dog to become more aggressive, especially if it feels threatened. Dogs that are punished for showing warning signs of aggression, like growling, may learn to skip those warnings and go straight to more serious aggressive behaviors, like biting.

- **Practical Example**: A dog that growls when it feels threatened may be punished for growling, leading it to skip the warning growl and bite in the future when it feels threatened again.

## Building Trust and Confidence

One of the key benefits of positive reinforcement is its ability to build trust and confidence in aggressive or fearful dogs. By focusing on rewarding positive behavior and avoiding punishment, dogs learn to feel safe, secure, and confident in their environment. This trust-building process is especially important for dogs that have a history of fear-based aggression or anxiety.

## The Role of Positive Reinforcement

### 1. **Providing Predictability and Security**:

Many aggressive behaviors stem from a dog feeling insecure or uncertain about its environment. Positive reinforcement helps create a structured, predictable routine where the dog knows what to expect. When a dog understands that certain behaviors consistently lead to rewards, it becomes more confident in its actions and more trusting of its owner.

- **Practical Example**: A dog that is anxious around new people can be taught to approach calmly by rewarding it each time it remains calm in the presence of strangers. Over time, the dog will learn that staying calm leads to positive outcomes, reducing its anxiety and aggression.

### 2. **Reinforcing Calm Behavior:**

Positive reinforcement helps aggressive dogs learn that calm, controlled behavior is more rewarding than reactive or aggressive behavior. By consistently rewarding the dog for remaining calm in situations that would normally trigger aggression, the dog's confidence grows as it learns to handle stressful situations more effectively.

- **Practical Example**: If a dog is reactive to other dogs on walks, rewarding it for calm behavior when another dog approaches teaches the dog that staying calm leads to treats or praise. Over time, the dog will become more confident and less reactive in these situations.

### 3. **Creating Positive Association:**

Positive reinforcement is particularly effective for dogs that have had negative experiences in the past. By pairing formerly stressful or scary situations with positive experiences (like treats or praise), the dog begins to form new, positive associations with those situations. This can help reduce aggressive behavior and build trust over time.

- **Practical Example**: If a dog has a history of being afraid of loud noises, rewarding the dog with treats or playtime during thunderstorms can help it form positive associations with the noise. Over time, the dog will feel less anxious and more confident during storms.

### 4. Encouraging Independent Decision-Making:

Positive reinforcement encourages dogs to think for themselves and make positive choices. When dogs learn that they can control their environment through their behavior (for example, sitting calmly leads to treats), they become more confident in their ability to navigate the world. This confidence reduces fear-based aggression, as the dog learns it can manage stressful situations.

- **Practical Example**: Teaching a dog to approach strangers calmly, rather than barking or lunging, allows the dog to feel in control of its actions. Over time, the dog will feel more confident and less fearful when encountering new people.

## Creating a Reward Structure

One of the most important aspects of positive reinforcement training is creating a structured reward system. Not all rewards are equal, and using the right type of reward at the right time can make a significant difference in your dog's progress. By establishing a clear reward hierarchy and using it consistently, you can reinforce desired behaviors and help your dog understand what is expected.

## How to Establish and Utilize a Reward?

A reward hierarchy involves categorizing rewards based on their value to the dog. High-value rewards are reserved for particularly challenging situations, while lower-value rewards can be used for easier tasks or everyday behavior. By using a reward hierarchy, you can motivate your dog more effectively and reinforce behaviors based on their difficulty.

1. **Determine What Your Dog Values**:

Every dog is different, so it's important to figure out what motivates your dog the most. For some dogs, food is the ultimate reward, while others may prefer a favorite toy, praise, or playtime. You can test different types of rewards to see what your dog responds to best.

- **Practical Example**: Try offering your dog a variety of rewards, like small pieces of chicken, a favorite ball, or verbal praise, to see which one gets the most enthusiastic response. Use this information to create your reward hierarchy.

**2. Create a Reward Hierarchy:**

Once you know what your dog values most, you can create a reward hierarchy to effectively reinforce different behaviors. A reward hierarchy is typically divided into three tiers:

- **High-Value Rewards**: These are the most coveted rewards and should be used sparingly for the most challenging situations or behaviors. High-value rewards might include special treats like chicken, cheese, or a favorite toy. These rewards are reserved for moments when your dog is performing a particularly difficult behavior, such as staying calm around a major trigger or successfully navigating a stressful situation.

  - **Practical Example**: If your dog struggles with leash reactivity toward other dogs, reserve high-value treats like chicken for moments when your dog remains calm as another dog approaches. This helps emphasize that staying calm during challenging encounters results in the best rewards.

- **Medium-Value Rewards**: These rewards are still motivating but not as irresistible as the high-value ones. Medium-value rewards might include your dog's regular treats or brief play sessions. These rewards can be used for behaviors that your dog has already learned but still needs reinforcement for, such as staying focused on walks or sitting on command.

- ○ **Practical Example**: Use medium-value rewards when your dog successfully follows basic commands like "sit" or "stay" during a mildly distracting environment, like your backyard. This reinforces good behavior in less stressful situations.

- **Low-Value Rewards**: These rewards are everyday reinforcements, such as verbal praise or a pat on the head. Low-value rewards can be used to maintain already established behaviors that your dog performs reliably, like sitting before meals or coming when called in a low-distraction environment.

- ○ **Practical Example**: If your dog consistently sits before meals, offering a quick "Good dog!" or a scratch behind the ears is sufficient to maintain this behavior without needing high-value treats.

### 3. Match the Reward to the Challenge:

Once you've established a reward hierarchy, use it strategically based on the difficulty of the behavior and the situation. Reserve high-value rewards for behaviors that require more effort or self-control, while low- and medium-value rewards can be used for simpler tasks. This approach keeps your dog motivated and helps it understand that more difficult tasks result in better rewards.

- **Practical Example**: If your dog is learning to stay calm around loud noises (like fireworks), use high-value rewards to reinforce calm behavior in these highly stressful situations. For less challenging scenarios, such as sitting before going outside, use medium- or low-value rewards to maintain good habits.

### 4. Fade Out Rewards Gradually:

As your dog becomes more proficient in its behavior, you can gradually reduce the frequency of rewards. This process, known as "fading," helps ensure that your dog's behavior becomes more reliable without needing constant reinforcement. However, it's important to keep rewarding your dog occasionally, so it doesn't lose motivation.

- **Practical Example**: If your dog has mastered staying calm around other dogs on walks, you can start reducing the frequency of high-value treats. Instead of giving a treat every time your dog passes another dog, you might reward it every other time or after a particularly challenging encounter.

**5. Incorporate Life Rewards:**

Life rewards are rewards that come naturally during the course of a day, such as getting to go for a walk, playing with a favorite toy, or receiving attention. Incorporating life rewards into your training can help reinforce positive behavior in everyday situations without relying solely on treats.

- **Practical Example**: If your dog sits patiently at the door before a walk, the reward could be the walk itself. By associating the walk with good behavior (like sitting calmly), your dog learns that it must behave to earn access to things it enjoys.

Positive reinforcement is an effective, humane way to train dogs, especially those dealing with aggression or anxiety. By focusing on rewarding desired behavior rather than punishing unwanted behavior, dogs learn to associate good choices with positive outcomes.

This method builds trust and confidence, which is especially important for aggressive dogs that may have underlying fear or insecurity driving their behavior.

By establishing a reward hierarchy, using high-value rewards strategically, and focusing on consistency, you can motivate your dog to make better choices and reinforce those behaviors over time.

Positive reinforcement not only helps reduce aggression and improve behavior but also strengthens the bond between you and your dog, creating a more harmonious and enjoyable relationship.

In the long run, the time and effort invested in reward-based training will pay off in a dog that is confident, well-behaved, and capable of handling even the most challenging situations with calmness and control.

# Chapter 9

# Management Strategies for Aggression

Aggressive behavior in dogs is often a manifestation of underlying stress, fear, or frustration. Addressing it requires not only behavior modification and training but also effective management strategies to keep both the dog and those around it safe during the training process.

Management is crucial in preventing the escalation of aggressive behaviors, providing a controlled environment where a dog can learn without being overwhelmed by its triggers.

In this chapter, we will explore the importance of management, the tools necessary to ensure safety, and how to create a safe and stress-free environment for your dog's rehabilitation.

## Why Management is Crucial

Management refers to the process of controlling the dog's environment to prevent aggressive outbursts and create a setting where training can be successful. While behavior modification is key to changing the underlying causes of aggression, management strategies ensure safety and control in the meantime, helping prevent situations that may lead to escalation.

## The Importance of Management

### 1. Preventing Aggressive Outbursts:

One of the primary goals of management is to prevent situations where the dog's aggressive behaviors could be triggered. Every time a dog engages in aggressive behavior, such as barking, growling, or biting, it reinforces those actions, making the behavior more ingrained. Management reduces the chances of the dog encountering these triggers before it's ready to cope with them, preventing negative reinforcement of aggression.

- **Practical Example**: If a dog is aggressive toward other dogs, avoiding high-traffic dog parks or busy streets while working on desensitization can prevent aggressive outbursts. By controlling the environment, you prevent the dog from becoming overwhelmed and reactive.

### 2. Ensuring Safety During Rehabilitation:

Safety is a top priority when managing aggressive dogs. Without proper management, there is a higher risk of the dog harming others or itself during the training process. Tools like es, harnesses, and muzzles can help reduce the risk of injury while the dog learns to control its behavior.

- **Practical Example**: A dog that is aggressive toward strangers can wear a muzzle during walks or when visitors come to the house. This ensures that the dog cannot bite, while still allowing it to observe and learn from its environment.

### 3. Creating an Optimal Learning Environment:

Management allows you to create an environment that's conducive to learning. When a dog feels safe and secure, it's more receptive to training and behavior modification. In contrast, if the dog is constantly exposed to triggers and stress, it's less likely to be able to focus on learning new behaviors.

- **Practical Example**: A dog that is reactive to loud noises can benefit from quiet training sessions in a low-distraction environment. Once the dog builds confidence in a controlled setting, it can gradually be exposed to more challenging situations.

#### 4. Preventing Setbacks:

Consistency is critical in behavior modification. Every time the dog experiences a trigger and reacts aggressively, it reinforces that aggression is an appropriate response. Management helps prevent setbacks by reducing the frequency of these reactions, allowing the dog to build positive associations during controlled training.

- **Practical Example**: A dog with food aggression can be fed in a separate room from other pets or people, preventing any confrontational situations. This management approach helps maintain a calm and positive environment, ensuring that the dog doesn't have the opportunity to guard resources aggressively.

## Tools for Management

When dealing with aggressive behaviors, various tools can help you safely manage the dog's environment. These tools are not meant to be used as long-term solutions but as temporary aids to keep everyone safe while the dog undergoes training.

## Using Physical Barriers, Crates, and Muzzles to Ensure Safety

### 1. Crates:

Crates can serve as safe spaces for dogs, giving them a place to retreat when they are feeling stressed or overwhelmed. A crate provides a controlled, enclosed environment where the dog can relax without the risk of encountering triggers.

Crate training is especially useful for dogs that are aggressive toward guests, other animals, or during specific times, like feeding.

- **Practical Example**: If a dog is aggressive toward visitors, it can be placed in a crate in a quiet room during social gatherings. This prevents the dog from reacting aggressively while also giving it a sense of security. Over time, you can work on desensitizing the dog to visitors while it remains in the crate, gradually building positive associations.

### 2. Baby Gates and Playpens:

Baby gates and playpens are useful for creating physical barriers within the home, allowing you to control the dog's access to certain areas. These barriers help keep the dog separated from potential triggers without isolating it completely. Gates can be used to block off rooms where other pets or children are present, giving the dog its own space.

- **Practical Example**: If a dog is aggressive toward other pets, you can use baby gates to separate the dogs while allowing them to see and smell each other from a distance. This slow introduction helps reduce tension and aggression without risking a direct confrontation.

### 3. Muzzles:

Muzzles are an important safety tool for aggressive dogs, especially in situations where biting is a concern. While some owners may feel hesitant about using a muzzle, it's a helpful management tool that allows the dog to interact with its environment safely. Muzzles should always be introduced gradually and paired with positive reinforcement to ensure the dog feels comfortable wearing them.

- **Training Tip**: Start by letting the dog sniff and investigate the muzzle, offering treats and praise for calm behavior. Gradually increase the amount of time the dog wears the muzzle, rewarding it each time. Eventually, the dog will associate the muzzle with positive experiences, reducing any anxiety it may have.

- **Practical Example**: A dog that has a history of biting can wear a muzzle during walks or in public places. This allows the dog to experience the environment while ensuring the safety of others. At the same time, the dog can undergo training to address the underlying causes of its aggression.

**4. Leashes and Harnesses:**

For dogs that are aggressive during walks or in public spaces, a sturdy leash and harness are essential. A harness provides more control over the dog's movements without putting pressure on its neck, reducing the likelihood of escalating aggressive behavior. Front-clip harnesses are especially useful for dogs that tend to pull or lunge.

- **Practical Example**: If a dog is reactive toward other dogs while on a leash, using a front-clip harness can help reduce pulling and allow the owner to maintain better control. The leash provides a physical boundary, while the harness prevents the dog from gaining momentum when lunging.

## Safe Management in Public Spaces and the Home

### 1. Managing Public Interactions:

When walking an aggressive or reactive dog in public, it's important to manage its interactions with other people and animals. Avoid crowded areas where the dog is likely to encounter multiple triggers, and always maintain control of the dog with a leash and harness. If necessary, use a muzzle for added safety.

- **Practical Example**: If you know your dog is reactive toward other dogs, plan walks during quieter times when fewer dogs are likely to be around. Keep your distance from potential triggers and use positive reinforcement to reward calm behavior. Over time, you can gradually expose the dog to more public situations as it becomes more comfortable.

2. Safe Management at Home:

In the home, it's important to create boundaries and establish safe spaces for aggressive dogs. This may involve using crates, baby gates, or designated areas where the dog can retreat when feeling overwhelmed. Ensuring that the dog has its own space reduces the risk of confrontations with other pets or family members.

- **Practical Example**: If a dog shows aggression toward children, set up a designated area in the home where the dog can relax without being disturbed. Teach children to respect the dog's space and avoid approaching it when it's in its safe zone. This management strategy helps prevent accidents while the dog undergoes behavior modification training.

**3. Leash Training for Controlled Walks:**

If a dog is reactive on walks, leash training is essential to managing the situation. Practice loose-leash walking and reward the dog for staying calm and focused on you. Use a front-clip harness to discourage pulling, and avoid tense situations where the dog may become overly aroused.

- **Practical Example**: If you encounter another dog during a walk and your dog starts to react, calmly turn and walk in the opposite direction while keeping the leash loose. Avoid pulling on the leash, as this can increase the dog's frustration and reactivity. Reward your dog when it stays calm and redirects its attention to you.

## Creating a Safe Environment

Creating a safe and stress-free environment is one of the most important aspects of managing an aggressive dog. A calm environment not only helps reduce stress and anxiety for the dog but also facilitates the learning process, making behavior modification more effective.

## How to Create a Safe and Stress-Free Environment?

1. **Reduce Environmental Stressors**:

Identifying and minimizing stressors in the dog's environment can go a long way in reducing aggression. Common stressors include loud noises, crowded spaces, and unpredictable interactions with people or other animals. Creating a quieter, more predictable environment helps the dog feel secure, making it easier to focus on training.

- **Practical Example**: If a dog is reactive to loud noises, consider using white noise machines or calming music to drown out disruptive sounds. Additionally, avoid taking the dog to busy, noisy areas until it has made significant progress in its behavior modification.

2. **Establish Clear Boundaries:**

Dogs thrive in environments where they understand the rules and boundaries. Setting clear boundaries helps prevent situations that could trigger aggression, such as unexpected interactions with other pets or family members. By creating structure in the dog's daily life, you can reduce the dog's anxiety and help it feel more in control, which in turn decreases aggressive responses.

- **Practical Example**: If a dog is aggressive around food, establish clear feeding boundaries. Feed the dog in a separate space from other pets, and avoid allowing anyone to approach the dog while it's eating. By creating this clear boundary, the dog will feel more secure and less likely to guard its food aggressively.

3. **Provide a Safe Space:**

Every dog needs a safe space where it can retreat when feeling stressed or overwhelmed. This can be a crate, a bed in a quiet room, or a specific area of the house where the dog knows it will not be disturbed. Having a dedicated safe space gives the dog a sense of security and control, reducing the likelihood of aggressive behavior.

- **Practical Example**: A dog that becomes aggressive around visitors can benefit from having a crate in a quiet room. When guests arrive, the dog can retreat to its crate, where it feels safe. Over time, you can work on desensitizing the dog to visitors by rewarding calm behavior from within its safe space.

### 4. Establish Routines:

Dogs thrive on routine, and having a predictable schedule can help reduce anxiety and prevent aggressive outbursts. Feeding times, walks, playtime, and rest periods should happen at consistent times each day. A structured routine helps the dog feel more secure and reduces the uncertainty that can lead to aggression.

- **Practical Example**: If a dog becomes anxious or aggressive when it doesn't know when its next meal or walk is coming, establishing a set routine can alleviate that anxiety. Feeding the dog at the same time every day and going for walks on a predictable schedule helps create a sense of stability.

### 5. Use Calming Tools and Aids:

Some dogs may benefit from calming aids, especially those that are prone to anxiety-driven aggression. Calming tools like pheromone diffusers, anxiety wraps (such as ThunderShirts), and calming supplements can help reduce stress in certain situations, making it easier for the dog to remain calm during training and rehabilitation.

- **Practical Example**: A dog that becomes anxious during thunderstorms or fireworks can benefit from a calming wrap or pheromone diffuser in the home. These tools help create a more relaxed environment, reducing the likelihood of aggressive behavior triggered by stress.

### 6. Exercise and Mental Stimulation:

Providing regular physical exercise and mental stimulation is crucial for reducing aggression in dogs. A dog that is bored or pent-up is more likely to exhibit aggressive behaviors. Daily exercise, puzzle toys, and interactive play sessions can help channel the dog's energy in positive ways, reducing frustration and the likelihood of aggression.

- **Practical Example**: If a dog tends to become aggressive after long periods of inactivity, increasing the amount of physical exercise and mental stimulation can help. Daily walks, fetch, and puzzle toys that engage the dog's mind can help expend energy and keep the dog calm and content.

Management strategies play a critical role in helping aggressive dogs navigate their world in a safe and controlled manner. While behavior modification is essential for addressing the root causes of aggression, management ensures safety and prevents escalation during the training process.

By using tools like crates, muzzles, and physical barriers, owners can prevent aggressive outbursts and create a safe environment where the dog can focus on learning new behaviors.

Additionally, creating a structured, predictable environment and reducing stressors are key to helping aggressive dogs feel secure. Whether through establishing routines, providing safe spaces, or using calming tools, these strategies help lay the foundation for successful rehabilitation.

In the long run, effective management not only keeps everyone safe but also helps the dog build confidence and trust, making it more receptive to training and less prone to aggressive behavior. With patience, consistency, and the right management tools, even the most aggressive dogs can learn to navigate the world with greater calm and control.

# Chapter 10

# Socialization and Exposure

S ocialization is a crucial part of any dog's development, but it's especially important for reactive dogs. For dogs that display aggressive or fearful behaviors, the process of safely exposing them to new people, places, and animals can be challenging.

Socialization helps dogs become more comfortable in unfamiliar environments and reduces the likelihood of negative reactions when encountering new stimuli.

This chapter focuses on controlled socialization, creating positive associations, and the importance of slow, steady progress to ensure successful socialization without overwhelming the dog.

## Controlled Socialization

For reactive dogs, unstructured or overwhelming socialization can do more harm than good. Controlled socialization allows the dog to be exposed to new experiences in a way that minimizes stress and fear, promoting positive behavior and learning.

Unlike the typical off-leash dog park scenario or random interactions on the street, controlled socialization involves carefully managing the dog's environment to ensure that exposure to new people, places, and animals is done gradually and at a pace the dog can handle.

## How to Safely Expose a Reactive Dog?

1. **Start in a Calm, Low-Distraction Environment**:

The first step in socializing a reactive dog is to choose an environment where the dog is least likely to be overwhelmed. This might be a quiet park or a friend's backyard where you can control the number of people or animals present. Starting in a calm setting allows the dog to experience new stimuli without feeling too anxious or reactive.

- **Practical Example**: If your dog is reactive to other dogs, begin by taking walks in a quiet neighborhood or park where you can keep your distance from other dogs. Gradually, as the dog becomes more comfortable, you can expose it to slightly busier areas, always maintaining control over the environment.

**2. Use Distance as a Buffer:**

Distance is one of the most important factors in managing socialization for reactive dogs. By keeping the dog at a safe distance from its triggers, you prevent it from becoming overwhelmed and reactive. As the dog becomes more comfortable, you can gradually reduce the distance, but the key is to work within the dog's comfort zone.

- **Practical Example**: If your dog is reactive to strangers, start by allowing it to observe people from a distance where it remains calm. Over time, you can reduce the distance between the dog and people as it learns to remain relaxed in their presence.

**3. Monitor Body Language:**

One of the most important aspects of controlled socialization is paying close attention to your dog's body language. Signs of stress, such as lip licking, yawning, or pacing, indicate that the dog may be feeling uncomfortable or overwhelmed.

If you notice these signs, it's important to increase the distance between your dog and the trigger or remove the dog from the situation.

- **Practical Example**: If your dog starts showing signs of stress when another dog approaches, such as stiffening or avoiding eye contact, it's time to increase the distance. Take a few steps back and give your dog space to relax.

### 4. Keep Initial Interactions Short:

When exposing a reactive dog to new situations, it's important to keep the initial interactions short and manageable. Prolonged exposure to a stressful situation can lead to a reactive outburst or increase the dog's anxiety. By starting with short interactions, you help the dog build confidence without becoming overwhelmed.

- **Practical Example**: If your dog is meeting a new person for the first time, allow the interaction to last only a few minutes, then give the dog a break. Over time, you can increase the length of the interactions as the dog becomes more comfortable.

### 5. Leashed Encounters:

During socialization, keeping your dog on a leash provides you with control and ensures that interactions don't escalate. Leashed encounters allow you to manage the distance between your dog and new stimuli and give you the ability to intervene if the dog becomes too reactive.

- **Practical Example**: When introducing your dog to another dog, keep both dogs on leashes. Allow them to sniff and interact briefly, then separate them before any tension arises. Gradually increase the length of the interactions as both dogs show positive, calm behavior.

### 6. Practice Patience:

Reactive dogs often need more time to adjust to new situations than other dogs. It's important to be patient and understand that progress may be slow. Rushing the process or forcing the dog into uncomfortable situations can set back its progress. Instead, focus on small victories and gradual improvements.

- **Practical Example**: If your dog struggles with meeting new dogs, celebrate small progress, such as calmly walking past another dog without reacting, even if the dogs don't interact directly. This shows that the dog is making progress, even if it's slow.

## Creating Positive Associations

Creating positive associations is key to helping reactive dogs become more comfortable in new environments. The goal is to pair new experiences with something the dog enjoys, such as treats, praise, or play, so that the dog learns to associate unfamiliar stimuli with positive outcomes. This approach helps shift the dog's emotional response from fear or anxiety to calmness and curiosity.

## Techniques for Ensuring Positive Experiences

1. **Use High-Value Rewards**:

When socializing a reactive dog, it's important to use high-value rewards to reinforce calm, positive behavior. High-value rewards are treats or toys that your dog finds particularly motivating. These rewards help create strong positive associations with the new people, places, or animals the dog encounters.

- **Practical Example**: If your dog is reactive to other dogs, reward it with small pieces of chicken or cheese every time it remains calm in the presence of another dog. The high-value treat will help the dog associate other dogs with something positive.

2. **Pair Triggers with Positive Reinforcement:**
Positive reinforcement can be used to change your dog's emotional response to its triggers. By rewarding your dog every time it encounters a trigger without reacting, you teach the dog to associate the trigger with good things, like treats or praise.

- **Practical Example**: If your dog is reactive to children, have a friend's child stand at a distance while you reward your dog with treats for staying calm. Over time, the dog will learn that being around children means receiving rewards, reducing its reactive behavior.

### 3. Timing is Key:

The timing of the reward is crucial when creating positive associations. The reward must be given immediately after the dog displays the desired behavior (such as staying calm) so that the dog understands what it's being rewarded for. If there's a delay in the reward, the dog may not make the connection between the behavior and the reward.

- **Practical Example**: If your dog stays calm while a stranger approaches, reward the dog the moment it remains relaxed. Waiting too long to give the treat may confuse the dog, as it might not understand that the calm behavior was the reason for the reward.

### 4. Gradual Exposure and Reward:

Positive associations are best built gradually. Start with mild versions of the trigger and reward calm behavior. As the dog becomes more comfortable, increase the intensity of the exposure while continuing to reward the dog for staying calm.

- **Practical Example**: If your dog is reactive to loud noises, start by playing soft recordings of the sound (such as thunderstorms or fireworks) and rewarding the dog for remaining calm. Gradually increase the volume over time while continuing to reinforce calm behavior with rewards.

### 5. Incorporate Play and Fun:

For some dogs, play can be just as rewarding as treats or praise. Incorporating play into socialization sessions helps the dog associate new environments or interactions with positive, fun experiences. Play also serves as a great stress reliever and helps the dog burn off nervous energy.

- **Practical Example**: If your dog enjoys playing fetch, use a favorite toy as a reward during socialization. After a calm encounter with another dog, reward your dog with a brief game of fetch. This helps the dog associate social situations with enjoyable activities.

### 6. Keep the Dog Below Its Threshold:

It's important to avoid exposing the dog to situations that cause it to become overly stressed or reactive. This is known as staying below the dog's "threshold." If the dog is pushed too far and begins to react aggressively or fearfully, it's harder to create positive associations. Always work within the dog's comfort zone, rewarding calm behavior and gradually increasing exposure as the dog becomes more confident.

- **Practical Example**: If your dog starts barking or lunging when another dog comes within 10 feet, increase the distance until the dog can remain calm. Reward the dog for staying relaxed, and gradually work on reducing the distance as the dog becomes more comfortable.

## Slow and Steady Progress

Socializing a reactive dog requires patience and a slow, steady approach. Rushing the process or overwhelming the dog can lead to setbacks and reinforce negative behaviors. By taking things slow and allowing the dog to progress at its own pace, you can help it build confidence and learn to navigate new situations calmly.

## Emphasizing the Importance of Slow, Controlled Exposure

### 1. Start Small and Build Confidence:

When beginning the socialization process, start with small, manageable experiences that the dog can handle without becoming reactive. As the dog successfully navigates these situations, its confidence will grow, making it easier to handle more challenging scenarios later on.

- **Practical Example**: If your dog is reactive to new people, start by having one calm person enter the home for a brief visit. Reward the dog for remaining calm, and gradually increase the number of people or the length of the visit as the dog becomes more comfortable.

**2. Celebrate Small Victories:**

Progress with reactive dogs can sometimes feel slow, but it's important to celebrate every small win. Whether it's your dog staying calm while passing another dog on the street, or simply not reacting when a new person enters the home, these moments are signs of improvement and should be acknowledged.

- **Practical Example**: If your dog usually barks when someone rings the doorbell, but today it only barked once before calming down, that's progress worth celebrating. Reward your dog for this improved behavior, as it reinforces positive outcomes.

**3. Gradually Increase Exposure:**

As your dog becomes more comfortable in controlled socialization settings, you can begin to increase the level of exposure to new stimuli. This might mean reducing the distance between your dog and other dogs or people, exposing your dog to busier environments, or increasing the length of time your dog spends in new situations.

- **Practical Example**: If your dog has been successfully walking past other dogs at a distance of 30 feet, try reducing the distance to 25 feet in your next session. Continue to reward calm behavior and increase exposure gradually to prevent overwhelming the dog.

**4. Repeat and Reinforce:**

Repetition is key when it comes to building confidence and reducing reactivity in dogs. Each successful exposure to a new person, place, or animal helps reinforce calm behavior and gradually reduces the dog's anxiety. It's important to repeat these experiences frequently, ensuring that positive behavior becomes a habit.

- **Practical Example**: If your dog remains calm when a stranger walks by during one walk, repeat this exposure on subsequent walks. Over time, your dog will begin to generalize this calm behavior to all strangers, reducing reactivity overall.

## 5. Allow Your Day to Set the Pace:

Each dog is different when it comes to socialization, and it's important to allow your dog to progress at its own pace. Pushing too quickly or exposing your dog to too much too soon can lead to setbacks and increased anxiety. Watch your dog's body language and reactions carefully, and adjust the level of exposure based on how your dog is coping.

- **Practical Example**: If your dog shows signs of stress after a few minutes in a busy environment, don't force it to stay longer. Instead, give the dog a break, return to a quieter space, and try again another day. Progress might be slow, but allowing your dog to set the pace will lead to more lasting improvements.

## 6. Managing Expectations:

Socializing a reactive dog is not a quick fix, and it's important to manage your expectations. Progress will be gradual, and there may be setbacks along the way. Some dogs may never become fully comfortable in certain situations, but they can learn to manage their reactions and behave more appropriately. Focus on progress, not perfection.

- **Practical Example**: If your dog remains anxious around large groups of people, it might never feel entirely comfortable in crowded areas. However, if your dog can stay calm in smaller groups or when meeting individuals, that's significant progress and should be seen as a success.

Socializing a reactive dog takes time, patience, and careful management, but it is essential for helping your dog become more confident and comfortable in new environments.

By using controlled socialization techniques, creating positive associations, and allowing your dog to progress at its own pace, you can help reduce reactivity and foster positive behaviors.

The key to success is taking small, manageable steps and focusing on gradual improvements. Whether it's learning to walk calmly past other dogs or feeling more comfortable around new people, each positive experience builds your dog's confidence and helps it handle future challenges with greater ease.

By following these strategies, you will not only improve your dog's behavior but also strengthen the bond between you and your dog, creating a trusting relationship built on patience, understanding, and positive reinforcement.

# Chapter 11

# Advanced Training for Aggressive Dogs

T raining aggressive dogs requires patience, consistency, and a deep understanding of canine behavior.

As dogs progress in their behavior modification, it becomes essential to advance their training by replacing aggression with alternative behaviors, shaping new behaviors through positive reinforcement, and utilizing more advanced desensitization techniques for those dogs that need additional support.

This chapter will explore how to teach alternate behaviors, the role of behavioral shaping and capturing, and methods to intensify desensitization training for dogs requiring more focused rehabilitation.

## Teaching Alternate Behaviors

One of the most effective ways to address aggressive behavior is by teaching the dog to replace the aggressive response with a more appropriate behavior.

Instead of punishing the dog for its aggression, you encourage it to engage in a different action when faced with a trigger. By consistently reinforcing the new, acceptable behavior, the dog gradually learns that aggression is unnecessary and that there are better ways to respond to stressful situations.

## Replacing Aggression with New, Acceptable Behaviors

### 1. Identify the Trigger and the Reaction:

The first step in teaching alternate behaviors is to identify what triggers the dog's aggression and what the dog's specific reaction is. This could be anything from barking, growling, lunging, or snapping when encountering other dogs or people. Once you know the trigger and the behavior, you can begin to replace it with a new response.

- **Practical Example**: If a dog reacts aggressively when a stranger enters the home, the new behavior could be teaching the dog to go to a specific spot (like a crate or a mat) and sit calmly. This gives the dog an action to focus on rather than reacting with aggression.

### 2. Choose an Alternate Behavior:

The alternate behavior must be something that the dog can easily perform and that is incompatible with aggression. For instance, a dog that is sitting or lying down cannot be lunging or barking at the same time. Commands like "sit," "stay," "focus," or "go to place" are often used as alternate behaviors because they are straightforward and can be reinforced easily.

- **Practical Example**: A dog that tends to bark aggressively at other dogs during walks can be taught to focus on the handler instead. The "focus" command, where the dog makes eye contact with the owner, diverts attention away from the trigger and onto the handler.

### 3. Train the Behavior in a Calm Setting:

Before introducing the new behavior during stressful situations, it's important to first train it in a calm, distraction-free environment. Ensure that the dog understands the command and can reliably perform the behavior when asked. Reinforce the new behavior consistently with rewards like treats, praise, or toys.

- **Practical Example**: Start by training the "sit" command at home or in a quiet backyard. Once the dog can sit reliably on command, you can begin using this command during more challenging situations.

### 4. Introduce the Triggers Gradually:

Once the dog understands the alternate behavior, it's time to begin practicing it in the presence of the trigger. Start at a distance or in a situation where the dog can notice the trigger but remains below its reactivity threshold. Gradually increase exposure to the trigger while consistently reinforcing the alternate behavior.

- **Practical Example**: If your dog reacts aggressively to bicycles, start by exposing it to bicycles at a distance while asking for the "focus" command. Gradually reduce the distance between the dog and the bicycles as the dog learns to focus on you rather than reacting.

### 5. Reward the Desired Behavior:

Reinforce the new behavior by rewarding the dog every time it responds appropriately to the trigger. Over time, the dog will learn that staying calm or focusing on the handler leads to rewards, and the aggressive response will fade.

- **Practical Example**: If your dog successfully goes to its mat and remains calm when guests enter the home, reward it with a high-value treat. This positive reinforcement helps solidify the new behavior.

## Behavioral Shaping and Capturing

Behavioral shaping and capturing are advanced techniques used to teach dogs complex behaviors or fine-tune their responses. These methods rely on positive reinforcement and gradual steps to guide the dog toward desired behaviors. Shaping and capturing are especially useful for aggressive dogs because they allow the handler to reinforce small successes, even if the dog is still learning how to control its reactions.

## How to Shape New Behaviors?

### 1. **What is Shaping?**

Shaping involves breaking down a complex behavior into small, manageable steps and rewarding the dog for each incremental success. Instead of waiting for the dog to perform the entire behavior perfectly, you reinforce approximations of the behavior and gradually build up to the final goal. This method is particularly useful for teaching dogs behaviors that don't come naturally to them.

- **Practical Example**: If you want to teach a dog to go to a specific spot (like a mat) when someone knocks on the door, start by rewarding the dog for simply moving toward the mat. Gradually, you can shape the behavior by only rewarding the dog when it steps onto the mat, then when it lies down, and finally when it stays there calmly.

**2. Using Shaping to Address Aggression:**

Shaping is a great tool for teaching aggressive dogs to respond calmly to triggers. By breaking down the process of staying calm into small steps, you can gradually build up the dog's tolerance to stressful situations while reinforcing positive behaviors at each stage.

- **Practical Example**: If a dog becomes aggressive when approached by another dog, start by rewarding the dog for staying calm when the other dog is far away. As the dog remains calm, gradually reduce the distance between the two dogs, continuing to reward calm behavior at each step.

**3. What is Capturing:**

Capturing is a technique used to reinforce behaviors that the dog offers naturally, without being prompted by the handler. By marking and rewarding a behavior as it happens, you encourage the dog to repeat it in the future. This method is useful for teaching behaviors that you want the dog to perform on its own, such as lying down quietly or relaxing in its bed.

- **Practical Example**: If you want to teach your dog to lie down on command, wait until the dog naturally lies down on its own. As soon as it does, reward it with a treat and praise. Over time, the dog will learn that lying down leads to rewards and will start offering the behavior more frequently.

**4. Combining Shaping and Capturing:**

Shaping and capturing can be used together to teach a dog new behaviors and refine existing ones. Shaping helps guide the dog toward a specific goal, while capturing reinforces behaviors the dog offers naturally. This combination allows you to build complex behaviors gradually while also reinforcing spontaneous positive actions.

- **Practical Example**: If your goal is to teach your dog to settle on a mat during stressful situations, you can use shaping to guide the dog to the mat and lie down. Then, use capturing to reinforce moments when the dog chooses to go to the mat and lie down on its own.

## Advanced Desensitization Techniques

Desensitization is a fundamental part of behavior modification for aggressive dogs, and advanced techniques can take this process to the next level. While basic desensitization involves gradual exposure to a trigger at a low intensity, advanced desensitization focuses on fine-tuning the process, adding layers of complexity to help dogs overcome deeply ingrained fears or aggressive behaviors.

## How to Take Desensitization to the Next Level?

1. **Increase the Complexity of Triggers**:

As dogs become more comfortable with basic desensitization, you can begin to introduce more complex or intense versions of the trigger. This helps the dog build resilience and learn to handle increasingly challenging situations. However, it's important to do this gradually and to always stay within the dog's comfort zone.

- **Practical Example**: If a dog has been successfully desensitized to the sound of a doorbell at a low volume, gradually increase the volume and add other elements, such as having a person walk through the door after the bell rings. Continue rewarding the dog for remaining calm at each step.

### 2. Vary the Context:

Dogs often learn to respond to triggers in specific contexts, but they may struggle when the context changes. Advanced desensitization involves practicing in different environments and under varying conditions to help the dog generalize its calm behavior across multiple settings.

- **Practical Example**: If your dog has learned to stay calm when it sees other dogs at a park, try practicing in other locations, such as on a busy street or in a different neighborhood. This helps the dog learn that calm behavior is expected in any situation.

### 3. Pairing Desensitization with Counter-Conditioning:

Advanced desensitization often involves pairing the exposure to a trigger with counter-conditioning, where the dog is taught to associate the trigger with something positive, like treats or play. This combination strengthens the dog's emotional response to the trigger, making it easier for the dog to stay calm.

- **Practical Example**: If your dog is reactive to strangers, pair desensitization (exposing the dog to strangers at a distance) with counter-conditioning by giving the dog a treat every time it sees a stranger. Over time, the dog will begin to associate the presence of strangers with positive experiences.

### 4. Introduce Movement and Action:

For many dogs, triggers that involve movement (such as bicycles, cars, or running children) can be particularly challenging. Advanced desensitization involves gradually exposing the dog to moving stimuli while maintaining calm behavior. Start with slower or less intense movements and work your way up to more complex versions of the trigger.

### 5. Gradual Introduction of Moving Triggers:

Movement can amplify a dog's reactivity, so when incorporating motion into desensitization, start with slower, less intense movements. Once the dog is comfortable, gradually increase the speed or intensity of the movement.

- **Practical Example**: If your dog reacts aggressively to cyclists, start by having a cyclist ride slowly by at a significant distance. Gradually reduce the distance between the dog and the cyclist, and increase the speed of the bike as the dog learns to stay calm. Continue reinforcing calm behavior with treats or praise.

### 6. Layering Multiple Triggers:

Advanced desensitization can also involve exposing the dog to multiple triggers simultaneously. However, this must be done carefully to avoid overwhelming the dog. Start by introducing one trigger at a time and then gradually layer in additional triggers as the dog becomes more comfortable.

- **Practical Example**: If your dog is reactive to both loud noises and other dogs, start by exposing it to one trigger at a time. Once the dog is comfortable with each individual trigger, you can introduce both triggers together, such as walking past another dog while a loud car drives by. Reward calm behavior to help the dog learn to manage both triggers.

### 7. Using Distance and Time Effectively:

Distance and timing are key components of desensitization. As your dog progresses, experiment with shortening the distance between the dog and the trigger or increasing the duration of exposure. However, always monitor the dog's comfort level to ensure that you're not pushing it too quickly.

- **Practical Example**: If your dog is reactive to other dogs on walks, you might start by practicing desensitization at a distance of 30 feet. As the dog becomes more comfortable, gradually decrease the distance while maintaining short sessions. Over time, you can work on longer exposures at closer distances, always ensuring the dog remains calm.

### 8. Incorporate Real-Life Scenarios:

The ultimate goal of advanced desensitization is to prepare the dog for real-life encounters. After practicing in controlled settings, begin incorporating more real-world scenarios where the dog might encounter triggers unexpectedly. This prepares the dog for unpredictable situations and helps solidify the calm behaviors learned during training.

- **Practical Example**: Once your dog can remain calm around other dogs in controlled settings, start taking your dog to new places, like a dog-friendly park, where it will encounter dogs and people in a less predictable environment. Continue using desensitization techniques and rewarding calm behavior to help the dog succeed in these more complex scenarios.

Addressing aggression in dogs requires more than just basic obedience and socialization—it often demands advanced techniques that help dogs replace aggressive behaviors with calm, controlled alternatives.

By teaching alternate behaviors, using shaping and capturing techniques, and employing advanced desensitization, you can create long-lasting behavioral change in aggressive dogs.

Teaching alternate behaviors gives dogs an outlet for their aggression, while shaping and capturing help refine those behaviors into predictable, positive responses.

Advanced desensitization techniques, such as incorporating movement, layering multiple triggers, and practicing in real-world scenarios, are essential for dogs with more complex behavioral issues.

These strategies, when used in conjunction with positive reinforcement, patience, and consistency, help even the most reactive dogs develop calm, confident responses to their triggers.

The key to success in advanced training is gradual exposure, patience, and consistency.

By carefully managing your dog's environment, rewarding calm behavior, and progressively increasing exposure to challenging situations, you can help your dog overcome aggression and lead a more balanced, peaceful life.

Ultimately, the combination of training, desensitization, and positive reinforcement will strengthen the bond between you and your dog, paving the way
for a more harmonious and stress-free relationship.

# Chapter 12

# When to Seek Professional Help

While many dog owners can manage their dogs' behavior with consistent training and positive reinforcement, there are times when aggressive behavior requires the expertise of a professional dog trainer or behaviorist.

Knowing when to seek professional help can be critical to ensuring both the safety of the dog and others. This chapter will explore how to identify when a dog's behavior necessitates professional intervention, what to look for in a qualified trainer or behaviorist, and how to work collaboratively to achieve lasting results.

## When is Professional Help Necessary?

Aggression in dogs can range from mild and manageable to severe and dangerous. Sometimes, the signs are subtle, while in other cases, they're more obvious. Recognizing when you're dealing with a situation beyond basic home training is the first step in addressing aggressive behavior properly.

## How to Identify When a Dog's Behavior Requires the Intervention?

## 1. **Escalating Aggression**:

If your dog's aggression is worsening despite your best efforts to manage and train, it's time to consult a professional. Escalating aggression might present as increased frequency or intensity in aggressive behaviors, such as barking, lunging, or biting. When these behaviors go unchecked, they can become dangerous and more difficult to reverse.

- **Practical Example**: If your dog has moved from growling at strangers to lunging or attempting to bite, this escalation indicates that the problem may be beyond basic training and requires professional intervention.

## 2. **Aggression Toward Family Members:**

Aggression directed at family members is a serious issue that often requires the help of a professional behaviorist. Whether the aggression stems from resource guarding, fear, or dominance issues, it's important to address it immediately to prevent harm and preserve the trust between the dog and the family.

- **Practical Example**: If your dog growls or snaps at family members when approached while eating or resting, this behavior should be evaluated by a professional to prevent escalation to more serious aggression.

## 3. **Unpredictable or Sudden Aggression:**

Suppose your dog displays sudden, unpredictable aggression without a clear trigger. In that case, this may be a sign of an underlying issue that needs expert evaluation. Dogs that lash out unexpectedly can be dangerous because their behavior is difficult to anticipate. A professional can help identify triggers that may not be immediately obvious to the owner.

- **Practical Example**: If your dog appears to react aggressively out of the blue, such as biting a guest without warning, it's essential to have a behaviorist assess the situation. Unpredictable aggression can stem from fear, pain, or a lack of socialization.

4. Biting or Near-Biting Incidents:

Any instance of biting or near-biting should be taken seriously. Even if the bite doesn't break the skin or cause injury, it indicates that the dog has reached a high level of stress or fear and is using aggression as a last resort. Biting can quickly escalate into more severe aggression if not addressed by a professional.

- **Practical Example**: If your dog has bitten a visitor during an interaction or has come close to biting someone, it's time to involve a professional behaviorist or trainer. They can assess the underlying causes and work on behavior modification.

### 5. Aggression Toward Other Animals:

If your dog is consistently aggressive toward other dogs or animals, it may be difficult to manage social situations, such as walks, trips to the dog park, or visits to the vet. Professional help is often needed to ensure that your dog can safely interact with other animals or, at the very least, learn to tolerate their presence.

- **Practical Example**: If your dog growls, lunges, or fights with other dogs on walks or during playdates, working with a professional trainer who specializes in aggression is crucial for managing and reducing these behaviors.

### 6. Failed Attempts at Home Training:

If you've tried multiple training methods and have been unable to make progress, this may be a sign that professional help is needed. Sometimes, well-intentioned training efforts fail because the aggression is rooted in complex behavioral issues that require a more nuanced approach. A behaviorist or trainer can help assess the situation and create a tailored training plan.

- **Practical Example**: If you've been working on desensitization and counter-conditioning for weeks with little to no improvement, a professional can assess what might be going wrong and adjust the training techniques.

## Choosing the Right Professional

Once you've recognized that your dog's aggressive behavior requires professional intervention, the next step is finding the right trainer or behaviorist. Not all professionals are equipped to handle aggression, so it's important to find someone with the right experience, qualifications, and approach to dealing with aggressive dogs.

## What to Look for in a Dog Trainer?

### 1. **Certification and Credentials**:

When seeking professional help, it's important to look for trainers or behaviorists who are certified by reputable organizations. Certification ensures that the trainer has undergone formal education and training in dog behavior and uses science-based methods. Some well-known certifying organizations include the International Association of Animal Behavior Consultants (IAABC), the Certification Council for Professional Dog Trainers (CCPDT), and the Karen Pryor Academy.

- **Practical Example**: Look for trainers who have certifications such as CPDT-KA (Certified Professional Dog Trainer) or CDBC (Certified Dog Behavior Consultant). These professionals are more likely to have experience with complex behavioral issues like aggression.

### 2. **Experience with Aggression:**

Not all trainers are equipped to handle aggressive dogs, so it's important to find a professional who specializes in aggression. Ask potential trainers about their experience working with dogs that exhibit aggressive behaviors, and inquire about their success rates with similar cases.

- **Practical Example**: When interviewing a trainer, ask specific questions such as, "Have you worked with dogs that exhibit fear-based aggression?" or "Can you provide examples of cases where you helped a dog with aggression toward other dogs?"

### 3. **Positive Reinforcement Techniques:**

A good trainer or behaviorist should use positive reinforcement techniques, which focus on rewarding desirable behaviors rather than punishing unwanted ones. Punishment-based methods can often exacerbate aggression, so it's important to avoid trainers who rely on tools like shock collars or aversive techniques.

- **Practical Example**: Ask trainers about their training philosophy. Look for responses that emphasize reward-based techniques and building trust with the dog, rather than dominance or punishment.

### 4. Personalized Training Plans:

Each dog is unique, and a one-size-fits-all approach is unlikely to work for aggressive behavior. A qualified professional should create a personalized training plan based on your dog's specific triggers, environment, and history. Look for trainers who take the time to assess your dog thoroughly before recommending a course of action.

- **Practical Example**: A trainer who offers an initial consultation to observe your dog and discuss its behavior is more likely to develop a customized plan than someone who jumps straight into a generic training program.

### 5. Comfort and Communication:

It's important to feel comfortable with the trainer or behaviorist you choose, as you'll be working closely with them throughout the behavior modification process. The professional should be approachable, willing to answer questions, and clear in their explanations. Good communication is key to ensuring that you understand the training methods and can implement them at home.

- **Practical Example**: During your initial conversation, assess whether the trainer listens to your concerns and explains their approach in a way that you understand. If you feel rushed or unclear about the plan, it may not be the right fit.

### 6. Client References or Testimonials:

A reputable trainer or behaviorist should be able to provide references from past clients who have successfully worked with them on aggressive behavior. Testimonials can give you insight into the trainer's approach, communication style, and the outcomes of their training programs.

- **Practical Example**: Ask the trainer if they can share case studies or connect you with previous clients who dealt with similar aggression issues. This will give you a sense of whether the trainer is likely to be a good fit for your dog's needs.

## Working with a Trainer

Once you've chosen the right professional, the next step is to work collaboratively to address your dog's aggressive behavior. Successful training requires a strong partnership between the trainer and the owner. By maintaining clear communication and staying actively involved in the training process, you can help ensure progress.

## How to Collaborate Effectively with a Professional?

### 1. Be Honest About Your Dog's Behavior:

When working with a professional, it's important to be completely honest about your dog's behavior. Don't downplay incidents or hide certain behaviors out of fear of judgment. The trainer needs a full understanding of the problem to create an effective training plan.

- **Practical Example**: If your dog has bitten someone in the past, it's crucial to share this information with the trainer. Withholding details could lead to an incomplete training plan and put others at risk.

### 2. Follow Through with Homework:

Training doesn't just happen during sessions with the professional—it requires consistent effort at home. The trainer will likely provide you with exercises and homework to reinforce the lessons learned during the sessions. Following through with this homework is essential for your dog's progress.

- **Practical Example**: If the trainer asks you to practice desensitization exercises with your dog between sessions, make sure to set aside time each day to complete the exercises. Consistency is key to making progress.

### 3. Be Patient with the Process:

Behavior modification, especially with aggressive dogs, takes time. It's important to be patient and not expect immediate results. There may be setbacks along the way, but with persistence and dedication, progress is achievable.

- **Practical Example**: If your dog has been reactive for years, it's unlikely that a few training sessions will completely resolve the issue. Stay committed to the long-term plan, and trust the process.

### 4. Stay in Communication with the Trainer:

Regular communication with the trainer is crucial to tracking progress and adjusting the training plan as needed. If you encounter new challenges or notice changes in your dog's behavior, share this information with the trainer so they can provide guidance and modify the approach if necessary.

- **Practical Example**: If your dog's aggression worsens in a specific situation (such as encountering new dogs), inform the trainer immediately. They can help you troubleshoot and adjust the training methods accordingly.

### 5. Celebrate Small Wins:

Progress with aggressive behavior can be slow, but every small improvement is a step in the right direction. Celebrate small wins along the way, such as your dog staying calm in a situation that used to trigger aggression. These victories build confidence and help you stay motivated.

- **Practical Example**: If your dog successfully walks past another dog without reacting for the first time, celebrate that progress with your trainer. This milestone shows that the training is working, even if there's still more work to be done.

Addressing aggressive behavior in dogs can be challenging, but professional help is often necessary to ensure the safety and well-being of both the dog and its surroundings. Recognizing when it's time to involve a trainer or behaviorist, choosing the right professional, and working collaboratively are all key components of a successful behavior modification plan.

By seeking out qualified, experienced professionals who specialize in aggression, dog owners can access the tools, guidance, and support needed to transform their dog's behavior. With patience, consistency, and expert help, even the most aggressive dogs can learn to manage their emotions and respond more calmly to the world around them.

# Chapter 13

# Stories and Long-Term Maintenance

T he journey to rehabilitate an aggressive dog is not always easy, but it's important to remember that success is achievable with the right approach, patience, and dedication.

This chapter explores real-life success stories of dogs who overcame aggression through consistent training and behavior modification. It also discusses how to maintain progress in the long term, prevent regression, and keep your dog's behavior in check through ongoing exercises.

Finally, we'll look at the importance of celebrating small wins to stay motivated and positive throughout the training journey.

## Real-Life Success Stories

Hearing about the success of other dogs that have overcome aggression can be incredibly inspiring for dog owners dealing with similar issues. These stories demonstrate that with the right training techniques, behavior modification, and commitment, even the most aggressive dogs can transform into well-behaved, confident companions.

## Example 1: Bella, the Rescue Dog with Fear-Based Aggression

Bella, a two-year-old rescue dog, had a traumatic start to life. She had been neglected and mistreated in her early months, which left her fearful and aggressive toward people, particularly men. Her owner, Sarah, adopted her from a shelter and was committed to helping Bella overcome her fear-based aggression. However, Bella would bark, growl, and even lunge at men who came too close, making daily walks and social interactions stressful.

Sarah sought help from a professional dog behaviorist who specialized in fear-based aggression.

Together, they developed a training plan that focused on desensitization and counter-conditioning. The goal was to gradually expose Bella to her triggers (men) in a controlled environment and reward calm behavior with high-value treats.

Progress was slow at first, but with consistent practice, Bella began to associate men with positive experiences. Over time, Bella's reactive behavior decreased, and she started showing curiosity instead of fear when men approached. Today, Bella can walk through the neighborhood without reacting aggressively, and she even accepts pets and treats from strangers. Sarah credits patience, consistency, and positive reinforcement for Bella's transformation.

## Example 2: Max, the Dog with Leash Aggression

Max, a four-year-old German Shepherd, was adopted from a shelter with a history of leash aggression. Every time Max saw another dog while on a walk, he would bark, lunge, and pull aggressively toward the other dog. His owners, Tom and Jessica, were dedicated to helping Max but felt overwhelmed by his behavior, which made walks stressful for everyone involved.

They decided to work with a professional dog trainer who specialized in leash reactivity. The trainer introduced a combination of desensitization and teaching alternate behaviors. Max was taught to "focus" on his owners whenever another dog was nearby. Using high-value treats, the trainer helped Max learn that staying calm and focused on Tom and Jessica during walks led to positive rewards.

Within a few months, Max's aggressive behavior on walks began to diminish. He no longer lunged at other dogs, and instead, he looked to his owners for guidance. Max's story is a testament to the power of consistent training, clear communication, and building trust between dog and owner.

## Example 3: Daisy, the Resource Guarder

Daisy, a three-year-old Labrador mix, had developed severe resource guarding behaviors. She would growl, snap, and even bite if anyone tried to approach her food bowl or favorite toys. Her family was concerned about the potential for harm, especially with young children in the home, so they sought help from a certified behaviorist.

The behaviorist worked with Daisy's family to implement a "trade-up" system, where Daisy learned to exchange her guarded items (food or toys) for something even better, like a high-value treat or a new toy. Over time, Daisy realized that giving up her resources didn't mean losing them but gaining something better.

Through consistent training and positive reinforcement, Daisy's resource guarding behavior began to diminish. She now calmly relinquishes her toys and food when asked, and her aggression has completely subsided. The family continues to practice these exercises to maintain the progress they've made, ensuring Daisy feels secure and comfortable in her home environment.

## Long-Term Maintenance

Training an aggressive dog doesn't end once the initial problem behaviors have been addressed. Long-term maintenance is crucial to ensure that the progress made during training continues. Without ongoing reinforcement, a dog can easily regress and return to its old behaviors. Therefore, it's essential to incorporate long-term strategies to maintain the positive changes in your dog's behavior.

## How to Maintain Progress and Prevent Regression

### 1. Consistency is Key:

One of the most important aspects of long-term maintenance is consistency. Dogs thrive on routine and predictability. To maintain your dog's progress, it's important to continue reinforcing the behaviors you've worked so hard to teach. This doesn't mean you need to train intensively every day, but regular reinforcement of good behavior is crucial.

- **Practical Example**: If you've trained your dog to stay calm around other dogs, continue to reward calm behavior during walks. Even after your dog has become comfortable, occasional rewards for good behavior will remind it of the positive consequences of staying calm.

### 2. Regular Training Sessions:

Incorporating short, regular training sessions into your dog's routine helps keep its skills sharp and reinforces positive behavior. These sessions don't need to be long—just 10 to 15 minutes a few times a week can make a big difference.

- **Practical Example**: Practice obedience commands like "sit," "stay," and "focus" during walks or playtime. Reinforce these commands with treats, praise, or play to keep your dog engaged and responsive.

### 3. Continue Socialization:

Regular exposure to new people, places, and animals is important for maintaining your dog's socialization skills. If a dog is not regularly exposed to different stimuli, it may become fearful or reactive again. Controlled socialization helps prevent this.

- **Practical Example**: Take your dog to new environments, such as parks, outdoor cafes, or dog-friendly events, to maintain its social skills. Continue to use positive reinforcement to reward calm behavior in these new settings.

### 4. Recognize Signs of Stress or Anxiety:

Even after successful training, dogs can experience stress or anxiety in certain situations. It's important to recognize the signs of stress, such as lip licking, yawning, or avoidance, and adjust the environment accordingly. If your dog starts showing signs of regression, revisit the training methods that worked in the past.

- **Practical Example**: If your dog begins to show anxiety around strangers again, return to desensitization exercises, gradually exposing your dog to people in a controlled manner while rewarding calm behavior.

### 5. Work on Impulse Control:

Impulse control exercises, such as "leave it" or "wait," help dogs practice self-control, which is especially important for aggressive dogs. Incorporating impulse control exercises into your dog's routine helps prevent impulsive, aggressive responses to triggers.

- **Practical Example**: Use the "wait" command before feeding your dog or before allowing it to go through a door. This reinforces the importance of self-control and helps prevent impulsive behaviors in other contexts.

## Celebrating Small Wins

Training an aggressive dog can feel like a long, challenging process, but it's important to celebrate every small win along the way. Recognizing and celebrating your dog's progress not only keeps you motivated but also reinforces positive behavior and strengthens the bond between you and your dog.

## How to Stay Motivated?

### 1. Acknowledge Incremental Progress:

Progress doesn't always happen in big leaps—it often comes in small, incremental steps. Celebrate these small improvements, whether it's your dog staying calm during a walk, reacting less intensely to a trigger, or obeying a command more reliably.

- **Practical Example**: If your dog used to bark aggressively at other dogs but now only barks once before calming down, this is a significant improvement. Celebrate this progress by rewarding your dog and acknowledging the hard work you've both put in.

### 2. Keep a Training Journal:

Maintaining a journal to track your dog's progress can be incredibly motivating. By recording your dog's behavior, the training techniques used, and the improvements you've seen, you'll be able to reflect on how far you've come and stay focused on your long-term goals.

- **Practical Example**: Write down notes after each training session, noting what went well and any challenges you encountered. Looking back at these entries will remind you of the progress made, even on days when it feels like things are moving slowly.

### 3. Reward Yourself:

Training an aggressive dog requires time, patience, and effort. It's important to acknowledge your role in your dog's progress and reward yourself for the dedication you've shown. This could be as simple as taking a break, treating yourself to something special, or celebrating with a friend who understands the journey.

- **Practical Example**: After a particularly successful training session, take some time to relax and do something you enjoy. Whether it's having a coffee, going for a walk without your dog, or celebrating with friends, rewarding yourself is just as important as rewarding your dog.

### 4. Strengthen Your Bond with Fun Activities:

Training shouldn't feel like a chore for you or your dog. Incorporate fun activities into your routine to strengthen the bond you've built during training.

Playtime, interactive games, or exploring new places together can help reinforce your connection and remind you why the hard work is worth it.

- **Practical Example**: After a successful training session, spend time playing your dog's favorite game or go on a new adventure together. This reinforces the idea that good behavior leads to positive experiences for both of you.

The stories of dogs like Bella, Max, and Daisy serve as powerful reminders that aggressive behavior can be transformed with the right approach, patience, and consistent effort.

While overcoming aggression is a significant achievement, long-term maintenance is just as important to ensure that progress is sustained and that your dog continues to thrive.

By incorporating ongoing training, consistent reinforcement, and regular socialization, you can prevent regression and keep your dog's behavior in check.

Celebrating small wins along the way not only boosts motivation but also strengthens the bond between you and your dog, making the training journey a rewarding experience for both.

# Chapter 14

# Conclusion

The journey from managing aggression to fostering calmness and control in dogs is a challenging but deeply rewarding process. It requires patience, dedication, and an unwavering commitment to positive training methods.

By understanding the root causes of aggression and implementing consistent behavior modification strategies, dog owners can guide their dogs toward healthier, more positive behaviors. This conclusion will summarize the key takeaways from the book, offer words of encouragement for dog owners, and provide resources for continued learning.

### Final Thoughts

Aggression in dogs is often misunderstood, and many owners feel frustrated or defeated when faced with their dog's challenging behaviors. However, as this guide has shown, aggression is a behavior that can be managed and modified through patience, proper training, and a deep understanding of the dog's triggers and needs.

Throughout this book, we've explored various types of aggression—whether fear-based, leash-related, resource guarding, or dog-to-dog aggression—and how to address them with practical strategies. The key to success lies in identifying the root cause of the behavior, applying consistent positive reinforcement, and implementing management tools to ensure safety during the training process.

Whether you've worked on desensitization, counter-conditioning, or teaching alternate behaviors, each step you've taken has moved your dog closer to a more balanced and confident state.

One of the most important lessons from this journey is that progress is not always linear. There will be setbacks, but each small step forward should be celebrated. The bond between you and your dog will strengthen as you continue to work together, and with time, dedication, and the right techniques, even the most reactive dogs can learn to manage their emotions and responses.

Remember, every dog is unique, and the journey to calmness and control will look different for each dog and owner. What matters most is your consistency and commitment to your dog's well-being. By embracing this journey with patience, you will be rewarded with a more peaceful, confident dog and a stronger relationship built on trust and mutual understanding.

**Words of Encouragement**

For dog owners facing the challenge of aggressive behavior, it can sometimes feel like there's no end in sight. The frustration of dealing with a reactive dog, combined with the pressures of daily life, can be overwhelming. However, it's essential to remember that change is possible, and every small victory brings you closer to your ultimate goal.

Your commitment to learning, practicing, and remaining patient is already a major step toward success. Dogs, like people, thrive on positive experiences and consistent feedback. With every calm encounter, every successful training session, and every moment of progress, you are teaching your dog that it can trust you to guide it through the world safely.

Many dog owners who face aggressive behavior initially feel isolated or unsure of where to turn, but by seeking help—whether from a professional trainer, support group, or educational resources—you're not only empowering yourself but also setting your dog up for long-term success. Continue to seek out knowledge, try new techniques, and adapt your approach as needed. Your efforts will make a lasting impact on your dog's life.

Take comfort in knowing that you are not alone on this journey. Many others have walked this path and successfully helped their dogs overcome aggression. Celebrate the small wins, and keep moving forward. Your dedication and love for your dog will pay off in ways you never imagined, leading to a more peaceful, fulfilling relationship.

**Resources for Further Learning**

For dog owners seeking to continue their education on managing and training aggressive or reactive dogs, there are many excellent resources available. Whether through books, online courses, or support groups, ongoing learning can provide you with new insights and techniques to further help your dog. Below are some recommended resources to explore:

**Suggested Reading:**

- **"The Culture Clash" by Jean Donaldson**: A must-read for dog owners, this book delves into dog behavior and training from a positive reinforcement perspective, helping owners understand the motivations behind a dog's actions.

- **"Mine! A Practical Guide to Resource Guarding in Dogs" by Jean Donaldson**: Focused on resource guarding, this book provides practical solutions for dealing with this specific type of aggression.

- **"Click to Calm: Healing the Aggressive Dog" by Emma Parsons**: A comprehensive guide on using clicker training to modify aggressive behavior, this book offers step-by-step instructions and case studies for owners working with reactive dogs.

- **"The Other End of the Leash" by Patricia McConnell**: This insightful book helps dog owners understand how human behavior impacts dog behavior and how to communicate more effectively with their pets.

**Websites and Online Courses:**

- **Karen Pryor Academy**: Known for its emphasis on positive reinforcement training, this academy offers a variety of online courses and webinars for dog owners and trainers alike. (www.karenpryoracademy.com)

- **International Association of Animal Behavior Consultants (IAABC)**: This organization provides resources, articles, and training guides for addressing complex behavior issues, including aggression. ( www.iaabc.org)

- **Fear Free Pets**: A resource that focuses on creating low-stress environments for pets, Fear Free Pets offers tools and courses for both pet owners and professionals working with anxious or fearful dogs. (www.fearfree pets.com)

**Support Groups and Forums:**

- **Reactive Dogs Facebook Group**: A supportive online community for dog owners dealing with reactivity and aggression. Members share advice, experiences, and offer emotional support.

- **Dog Aggression Support Network**: An online forum where dog owners can seek advice, share success stories, and discuss various approaches to dealing with aggression.

- **Meetup Groups**: Many cities have local groups for dog owners to meet and practice socialization in a controlled setting. These groups can be a great way to connect with others facing similar challenges.

**Final Thoughts**

Helping an aggressive or reactive dog requires time, effort, and a willingness to adapt. However, the rewards are immense. Not only will you see improvements in your dog's behavior, but you'll also build a stronger, more trusting bond with your pet. By remaining patient, consistent, and open to learning, you can guide your dog toward a calmer, more confident future.

Remember to celebrate every step forward—no matter how small—and to seek out support when needed. Your dedication and love for your dog will continue to make a difference in its life, and with each day, you'll see the positive effects of your hard work.

As you continue this journey, never stop learning, and always believe in your dog's ability to grow and improve. With the right approach, even the most challenging behaviors can be transformed, leading to a happier and more peaceful life for both you and your dog.

# Chapter 15

# Thank you!

Thank you so much for reading this book! Your support truly means the world to me. If you found the content helpful or insightful, I would be incredibly grateful if you could take a moment to leave a review on Amazon or Goodreads.

Your feedback helps others discover this book and gain from it just as you have. Reviews, even brief ones, make a big difference in reaching new readers and continuing to share valuable information.

Once again, thank you for your time, your thoughts, and for supporting this work!

Made in the USA
Las Vegas, NV
10 December 2024

13827458R00090